KU-350-067

THE UK TOWER VORTX
Dual Basket Air Fryer Cookbook

1200 Days Effortless and Yummy Recipes for Beginners and Advanced Users
to Master Your Smart Tower Dual Zone Air Fryer

Cara Roslin

Copyright © 2023 By Cara Roslin All rights reserved.

No part of this book may be reproduced, transmitted, or distributed in any form or by any means without permission in writing from the publisher except in the case of brief quotations embodied in critical articles or reviews.

Legal & Disclaimer

The content and information in this book is consistent and truthful, and it has been provided for informational, educational and business purposes only.

The illustrations in the book are from the website shutterstock.com, depositphoto.com and freepik.com and have been authorized.

The content and information contained in this book has been compiled from reliable sources, which are accurate based on the knowledge, belief, expertise and information of the Author. The author cannot be held liable for any omissions and/or errors.

Table of Contents

INTRODUCTION

Greetings, fellow food enthusiasts! Allow me to share with you the delightful journey of embracing the Tower Vortx Dual Basket Air Fryer - a kitchen marvel that has revolutionized my culinary experience and transformed my life!

As a passionate cook, I've always sought ways to create scrumptious and healthy meals for myself and my loved ones. The Tower Vortx Dual Basket Air Fryer has been my ultimate companion in this pursuit, bringing an array of benefits and ease to my cooking routine.

The Duo Basket Technology offers unparalleled versatility, presenting two generous 4.5L baskets that cater to both small and large portion cooking. Whether I'm whipping up a quick snack or preparing a feast for a gathering, this appliance accommodates it all. Imagine the joy of serving delicious, crispy, and wholesome meals, enough to feed up to 8 people, without breaking a sweat!

The Smart Finish function has become a game-changer for me, eliminating the hassle of juggling different cooking times. It synchronises the cooking process for both baskets, ensuring that all components of my meal are cooked to perfection simultaneously. No more worries about overcooking or undercooking; the Match Cook button ensures every element of my culinary masterpiece is flawlessly prepared.

The Tower Vortx Dual Basket Air Fryer's versatility extends beyond just air frying. With 10 pre-set meal classics, it has become my go-to appliance for roasting succulent meats, baking mouthwatering cakes, pies, and tarts, and even grilling juicy steaks like a seasoned chef. The pre-set options take away the guesswork, guaranteeing consistently fantastic results with every dish I prepare.

The impact on my energy consumption and expenses

has been truly remarkable. This air fryer operates efficiently, utilizing up to 70% less energy compared to conventional ovens. My energy bills have seen significant reductions, and I estimate saving up to £259 per year - now that's money well saved!

Cleaning and caring for the Tower Vortx Dual Basket Air Fryer is a breeze. Its user-friendly design makes it easy to maintain after each use. A quick wipe and gentle cleaning with hot water and a non-abrasive sponge keep it in top-notch condition, ready for my next culinary adventure.

Embracing this kitchen gem has been nothing short of a revelation. My cooking has reached new heights, and my meals have garnered admiration from friends and family alike. The Tower Vortx Dual Basket Air Fryer has not only enhanced my culinary creations but also freed up valuable time, making my life a whole lot easier.

So, fellow foodies, get ready to embark on an extraordinary culinary journey with the Tower Vortx Dual Basket Air Fryer. Embrace its versatility, savor the convenience, and witness the transformation it brings to your cooking and lifestyle. Get ready to unlock the true potential of this extraordinary kitchen companion and elevate your culinary experience to new heights!

Preset Functions and SYNC

Unleash the culinary potential of the Tower Vortx Dual Basket Air Fryer with its impressive array of 10 pre-set functions! Each function is designed to deliver mouthwatering dishes with just a touch of a button, taking the guesswork out of cooking and ensuring consistent, delicious results.

But that's not all - the Tower Vortx Air Fryer goes above and beyond with its innovative Match Cook and Smart Finish features. These ingenious functions elevate your cooking experience, allowing you to effortlessly create multi-course meals without the stress of juggling different cooking times. Let's dive into the magic that awaits you in the world of the Tower Vortx Dual Basket Air Fryer!

Fries: Crispy and golden fries are just a touch away! This pre-set function ensures perfectly cooked fries without the need for excessive oil, making them a guilt-free treat.

Meat: From juicy burgers to succulent chicken breasts, the Meat function delivers mouthwatering results every time, locking in the flavours while keeping the meat tender and moist.

Fish: Enjoy perfectly cooked fish without the hassle. The Fish pre-set function ensures delicate fish fillets come out flaky and flavourful with a crispy outer layer.

Prawn: Savor the taste of perfectly cooked prawns, whether as a standalone dish or a delightful addition to your favourite recipes.

Drumsticks: Get that finger-licking goodness with the Drumsticks function. Crispy on the outside and juicy on the inside, it's a favourite for both kids and adults.

Steak: Elevate your steak game with the Steak function. Achieve restaurant-quality results with the perfect sear and desired doneness every time.

Cake: Indulge in the joy of baking without the need for a traditional oven. The Cake pre-set function bakes delicious cakes, tarts, and pies to perfection.

Vegetables: Enjoy the natural flavours of vegetables with the Vegetables function. It ensures that your veggies are cooked just right, retaining their vibrant colours and nutritional value.

Pizza: Craving a crispy pizza crust? The Pizza pre-set function delivers a perfectly baked pizza, satisfying your pizza cravings with ease.

Reheat: Leftovers just got better with the Reheat function. Say goodbye to soggy microwave reheating; this function brings back the crispy texture and delicious taste to your favourite dishes.

Match Cook: The Match Cook feature of the Tower Vortx Dual Basket Air Fryer is a culinary blessing. Whether you're preparing the same food or different dishes with same cooking requirements, the Match Cook button comes to the rescue. Activating this function ensures that both baskets cook at the same temperature and for the same duration, guaranteeing perfectly synchronised results. Say goodbye to the hassle of coordinating multiple dishes or worrying about unevenly cooked meals. With Match Cook, your culinary creations will always be perfectly timed and ready to delight your taste buds. Enjoy the convenience and harmony of simultaneous cooking with this ingenious feature!

Smart Finish: Gone are the days of trying to time multiple dishes to finish cooking at the same time. With the Smart Finish function, the Tower Vortx Dual Basket Air Fryer does the work for you. This innovative feature detects the different cooking times in each basket and synchronises the cooking process, so both baskets finish cooking at the same time. Whether you're preparing a full meal or a variety of starters, Smart Finish guarantees perfectly cooked dishes without any guesswork or culinary acrobatics.

There you have it! The 10 pre-set functions, along with the Match Cook and Smart Finish features, make the Tower Vortx Dual Basket Air Fryer an exceptional kitchen companion, simplifying your cooking process and ensuring impressive results every time.

Advantages of the Tower Vortx Dual Basket Air Fryer:Advantages of the Tower Vortx Dual Basket Air Fryer:

Versatile Culinary Wizardry: The Tower Vortx Dual Basket Air Fryer is a true kitchen marvel with its 10 pre-set functions. From air frying to baking, grilling, roasting, and more, it caters to all your culinary desires, making it a versatile all-in-one appliance.

Healthier Indulgences: Savor your favourite fried treats guilt-free! The Tower Vortx Air Fryer uses up to 70% less oil, producing crispy and flavourful results without the excess fat, perfect for those seeking healthier meal options.

Effortless Meal Preparation: Say goodbye to complicated cooking routines. The Tower Vortx Air Fryer's intuitive design and pre-set functions take the guesswork out of cooking, making meal preparation a breeze for even the busiest of kitchens.

Cook for a Crowd: With its Duo Basket Technology, the Tower Vortx Air Fryer can simultaneously cook two separate dishes, ideal for entertaining guests or preparing multiple courses for family dinners.

Time and Energy Savings: Enjoy faster cooking times and lower energy consumption with the Tower Vortx Dual Basket Air Fryer. Its powerful performance ensures delicious meals in less time, while also being eco-friendly and cost-efficient.

Easy Cleanup: The non-stick baskets and grill plate make cleaning up a cinch. A quick wipe and gentle wash keep your air fryer in top-notch condition, ready for your next delightful creation.

Elevate Your Cooking Experience: Embrace the Tower Vortx Dual Basket Air Fryer and unleash your culinary creativity. From delectable starters to mouthwatering mains and scrumptious desserts, this appliance empowers you to become a master chef in your own kitchen.

In conclusion, the Tower Vortx Dual Basket Air Fryer has been a game-changer in my kitchen. With its versatile cooking options, healthier approach, and time-saving features, it has made meal preparation a breeze. Embrace the Tower Vortx Air Fryer and elevate your cooking experience to a whole new level of convenience and deliciousness. Happy cooking!

CHAPTER 1

Breakfast

Mustard Pork Meatballs

SERVES 4

| PREP TIME: 15 minutes
| COOK TIME: 15 minutes

225 g minced pork
1 onion, chopped
8 g fresh basil, chopped
5 ml honey
5 g Parmesan cheese, grated
5 g cheddar cheese, grated
1 tsp. mustard
1 tsp. garlic paste
salt and black pepper, to taste

1. Mix together all the ingredients in a bowl until well combined.
2. Make small equal-sized balls from the mixture.
3. When ready to cook, remove the grill plate from basket 1 then preheat the airfryer basket for three minutes by activating the automatic preheat key.
4. Put the meatballs into basket 1 and set the temperature to 200°C for 15 minutes then touch the start key to activate the airfryer. Halfway through cooking, carefully flip the meatballs over.
5. Transfer the meatballs to a plate. Serve warm.

Cinnamon Courgette Bread

SERVES 6

| PREP TIME: 15 minutes
| COOK TIME: 20 minutes

240 ml vegetable oil
375 g plain flour
3 eggs
100 g walnuts, chopped
300 g courgette, grated

400 g white sugar
10 g baking powder
8 g ground cinnamon
15 ml vanilla extract
1 tsp. salt

1. Grease two (18 x10 cm) loaf pans lightly.
2. Mix together the flour, baking powder, cinnamon and salt in a bowl.
3. Whisk together eggs with vanilla extract, sugar and vegetable oil in a bowl until well combined.
4. Stir in the flour mixture and gently fold in the courgette and walnuts.
5. Mix until well combined and transfer the mixture into the prepared loaf pans.
6. When ready to cook, remove the grill plates and preheat the airfryer baskets for three minutes by activating the automatic preheat key.
7. Place 1 loaf pan in each basket. Select the Match Cook key then set basket 1 to 160°C for 20 minutes, then touch the start key to activate the airfryer.
8. When cooking is complete, remove from the airfryer and place onto a wire rack to cool. Cut the bread into desired size slices and serve.

Tasty Toasts with Salmon

SERVES 4

| PREP TIME: 10 minutes
| COOK TIME: 6 minutes

4 bread slices
115 g smoked salmon
225 g ricotta cheese
40 g rocket
1 shallot, sliced
1 garlic clove, minced
1 tsp. lemon zest
¼ tsp. freshly ground black pepper

1. Preheat the airfryer baskets with the grill plates inserted for three minutes by activating the automatic preheat key.
2. Place 2 bread slices in a single layer in each basket. Select the Match Cook key and set basket 1 to 180°C for 6 minutes and touch the start key to activate.
3. Meanwhile, put the garlic, ricotta cheese and lemon zest in a food processor and pulse until smooth.
4. When the bread is ready, transfer the bread slices to a plate.
5. Spread the cheese mixture over each bread slice and top with salmon, rocket and shallot.
6. Sprinkle with black pepper to taste and serve warm.

Tomato and Mozzarella Bruschetta

SERVES 2

| PREP TIME: 5 minutes
| COOK TIME: 6 minutes

15 ml olive oil
6 small loaf slices
75 g tomatoes, finely chopped
85 g Mozzarella cheese, grated
3 g fresh basil, chopped

1. Preheat the airfryer baskets with the grill plates inserted for three minutes by activating the automatic preheat key.
2. Place 3 loaf slices in a single layer in each basket. Select the Match Cook key and set basket 1 to 180°C for 6 minutes and touch the start key to activate.
3. When the loaf slices have been cooking for 4 minutes, add the tomato, Mozzarella, basil, and olive oil on top and cook for a further 2 minutes until the cheese is melted.
4. When cooking is complete, serve warm.

Apple Walnut Muffins

MAKES 8 MUFFINS

| PREP TIME: 15 minutes
| COOK TIME: 12 minutes

120 g flour
70 g sugar
1 egg
180 g unsweetened apple sauce
40 g pancake syrup
40 g melted butter
5 g baking powder
1 g baking soda

30 g chopped walnuts
30 g diced apple
¼ tsp. salt
2 g cinnamon
¼ tsp. ginger
¼ tsp. nutmeg
½ tsp. vanilla extract

1. In a large bowl, stir together the flour, baking powder, baking soda, sugar, salt, cinnamon, ginger, and nutmeg.
2. In a small bowl, beat the egg until frothy. Add the syrup, butter, apple sauce, and vanilla and mix well.
3. Pour the egg mixture into the dry ingredients and stir just until moistened.
4. Gently stir in walnuts and diced apple.
5. Divide the batter among 8 parchment-paper-lined muffin cups.
6. When ready to cook, remove the grill plates and preheat the airfryer baskets for three minutes by activating the automatic preheat key.
7. Place 4 muffin cups in each basket. Select the Match Cook key then set basket 1 to 180°C for 12 minutes, then touch the start key to activate the airfryer. Cook until toothpick inserted in centre comes out clean.
8. Serve warm.

Sourdough Croutons

SERVES 2

| PREP TIME: 5 minutes
| COOK TIME: 6 minutes

15 ml olive oil
280 g cubed sourdough bread, 2.5 cm cubes
1 tsp. fresh thyme leaves
¼ tsp. salt
Freshly ground black pepper, to taste

1. Combine all the ingredients in a bowl.
2. When ready to cook, remove the grill plate from basket 1 then preheat the airfryer basket for three minutes by activating the automatic preheat key.
3. Put the bread cubes into basket 1 and set the temperature to 200°C for 6 minutes then touch the start key to activate the airfryer. Halfway through cooking, give the bread cubes a shake.
4. When cooking is complete, transfer the bread cubes to a plate. Serve warm.

Pitta and Pepperoni Pizza

SERVES 1

| PREP TIME: 10 minutes
| COOK TIME: 8 minutes

5 ml olive oil
1 pitta bread
15 ml pizza sauce
25 g grated Mozzarella cheese
6 pepperoni slices
¼ tsp. garlic powder
¼ tsp. dried oregano

1. Spread the pizza sauce on top of the pitta bread. Put the pepperoni slices over the sauce, followed by the Mozzarella cheese.
2. Season with garlic powder and oregano.
3. Preheat the basket 1 with the grill plate inserted for three minutes by activating the automatic preheat key.
4. Grease the grill plate with olive oil. Place pitta pizza in basket 1 and set the temperature to 180°C for 8 minutes then touch the start key to activate the airfryer.
5. When the pizza is ready, carefully remove from the airfryer with a silicone spatula. Serve warm.

Healthy Mushroom and Squash Toast

SERVES 4

| PREP TIME: 10 minutes
| COOK TIME: 15 minutes

15 ml olive oil
2 spring onions, sliced
1 red bell pepper, cut into strips
1 small yellow squash, sliced
225 g sliced button or chestnut mushrooms
4 slices bread
115 g soft goat cheese
30 g softened butter

1. Add the red pepper, spring onions, mushrooms, and squash in a medium bowl, and stir well.
2. Spread the butter on the bread slices.
3. When ready to cook, remove the grill plate from basket 1, then preheat the airfryer baskets for three minutes by activating the automatic preheat key.
4. Brush the vegetables with the olive oil and place into basket 1, set the temperature to 200°C and for 15 minutes then carefully place the bread slices onto the grill plate in basket 2, set the temperature to 180°C and for 6 minutes.
5. Select the Smart Finish key then touch the start key to activate the airfryer. Halfway through cooking, give the vegetables a shake.
6. When cooking is complete, transfer the bread slices to a plate. Top with the goat cheese and cooked vegetables. Serve warm.

Buttermilk Scones

MAKES 12 SCONES

| PREP TIME: 5 minutes
| COOK TIME: 7 minutes

250 g plain flour, plus more for dusting the work surface
85 g cold unsalted butter, cut into 15 g slices
180 ml buttermilk
15 g baking powder
1 g baking soda
10 g sugar
1 tsp. salt

1. In a large mixing bowl, combine the flour, baking soda, baking powder, sugar, and salt and mix well.
2. Cut in the butter with a fork until the mixture resembles coarse meal.
3. Add the buttermilk and mix until smooth.
4. Dust more flour on a clean work surface. Turn the dough out onto the work surface and roll it out until it is about 1 cm thick.
5. Using a 5-cm scone cutter, cut out the scones.
6. Preheat the airfryer baskets with the grill plates inserted for three minutes by activating the automatic preheat key.
7. Spray the grill plates with olive oil. Place half of the scones in a single layer in each basket. Select the Match Cook key and set basket 1 to 180°C for 7 minutes and touch the start key to activate.
8. When the scones are ready, transfer to a plate and serve warm.

Perfect Cheesy Eggs

SERVES 2

| PREP TIME: 10 minutes
| COOK TIME: 12 minutes

10 g unsalted butter, softened
4 large eggs, divided
55 g ham, sliced thinly
30 ml double cream
25 g Parmesan cheese, grated finely
2 g fresh chives, minced
⅛ tsp. smoked paprika
Salt and black pepper, to taste

1. Grease a 13 cm pie dish with butter.
2. Whisk together 1 egg with cream, salt and black pepper to taste in a bowl.
3. Place the ham slices in the bottom of the pie dish and top with the egg mixture.
4. Crack the remaining eggs on top and season with smoked paprika, salt and black pepper. Top evenly with Parmesan cheese and chives.
5. When ready to cook, remove the grill plate from basket 1 then preheat the airfryer basket for three minutes by activating the automatic preheat key.
6. Place the pie dish into basket 1 and set the temperature to 160°C for 12 minutes then touch the start key to activate the airfryer.
7. When cooking is complete, serve with toasted bread slices.

CHAPTER 2

Fish and Seafood

Cod with Asparagus

SERVES 2

| PREP TIME: 15 minutes
| COOK TIME: 20 minutes

2 (170 g) boneless cod fillets
6 g fresh parsley, roughly chopped
6 g fresh dill, roughly chopped
1 bunch asparagus
1 tsp. dried basil
20 ml fresh lemon juice
15 ml olive oil
Salt and black pepper, to taste

1. Mix the lemon juice, oil, basil, salt, and black pepper in a small bowl.
2. Combine the cod and ¾ of the oil mixture in another bowl.
3. Coat the asparagus with remaining oil mixture.
4. When ready to cook, remove the grill plate from basket 2 then preheat the airfryer baskets for three minutes by activating the automatic preheat key.
5. Place the cod carefully onto the grill plate in basket 1 and set the temperature to 180°C for 15 minutes. Put the asparagus into basket 2 and set the temperature to 200°C for 20 minutes then activate the Smart Finish key and touch the start key to activate the airfryer. Halfway through cooking, flip the cod and asparagus over.
6. When cooking is complete, serve the cod immediately with asparagus.

Breaded Flounder with Green Beans

SERVES 3

| PREP TIME: 15 minutes
| COOK TIME: 17 minutes

1 egg
3 (170 g) flounder fillets
100 g dry breadcrumbs
1 lemon, sliced
60 ml vegetable oil
225 g fresh green beans, trimmed and cut in half
15 ml soy sauce
5 ml sesame oil

1. Whisk the egg in a shallow bowl and mix the breadcrumbs and oil in another bowl.
2. Dip the flounder fillets into the whisked egg and coat with the breadcrumb mixture.
3. Mix the green beans, soy sauce, and sesame oil in a bowl and toss to coat well.
4. When ready to cook, remove the grill plate from basket 2 then preheat the airfryer baskets for three minutes by activating the automatic preheat key.
5. Place the flounder fillets onto the grill plate in basket 1 and set the temperature to 180°C for 17 minutes. Put the green beans into basket 2 and set the temperature to 200°C for 12 minutes then activate the Smart Finish key and touch the start key to activate the airfryer. Halfway through cooking, flip the flounder fillets and green beans over.
6. When cooking is complete, serve the flounder fillets and green beans with lemon slices.

Honey Salmon Fillets

SERVES 2

| PREP TIME: 10 minutes
| COOK TIME: 10 minutes

5 ml water
2 (100 g) salmon fillets
80 ml soy sauce
80 ml honey
15 ml rice wine vinegar

1. Mix all the ingredients in a small bowl except the salmon.
2. Reserve half of the mixture in a small bowl and coat the salmon in remaining mixture. Refrigerate, covered for about 2 hours.
3. Preheat the basket 1 with the grill plate inserted for three minutes by activating the automatic preheat key.
4. Place the salmon into basket 1 and set the temperature to 180°C for 10 minutes then touch the start key to activate the airfryer. Halfway through cooking, flip the salmon over.
5. Meanwhile, place the reserved marinade in a small pan and cook for about 1 minute.
6. When cooking is complete, transfer the salmon to a plate. Serve the salmon with marinade sauce and enjoy.

Paprika Tiger Prawns

SERVES 2

| PREP TIME: 10 minutes
| COOK TIME: 8 minutes

225 g tiger prawns
15 ml olive oil
½ tsp. old bay seasoning
¼ tsp. smoked paprika
¼ tsp. cayenne pepper
Salt, to taste

1. Mix all the ingredients in a large bowl until well combined.
2. When ready to cook, remove the grill plate from basket 1 then preheat the airfryer basket for three minutes by activating the automatic preheat key.
3. Put the prawns into basket 1 and set the temperature to 180°C for 8 minutes then touch the start key to activate the airfryer. Halfway through cooking, carefully turn the prawns.
4. When cooking is complete, transfer the prawns to a plate. Serve warm.

Super-Simple Scallops

SERVES 2

| PREP TIME: 10 minutes
| COOK TIME: 8 minutes

340 g sea scallops
15 g butter, melted
½ tbsp. fresh thyme, minced
Salt and black pepper, to taste

1. Mix all the ingredients in a bowl and toss to coat well.
2. Preheat the basket 1 with the grill plate inserted for three minutes by activating the automatic preheat key.
3. Place the scallops into basket 1 and set the temperature to 180°C for 8 minutes then touch the start key to activate the airfryer. Halfway through cooking, flip the scallops over.
4. When cooking is complete, transfer the scallops to a plate. Serve warm.

Garlic-Lemon Tilapia

SERVES 4

| PREP TIME: 5 minutes
| COOK TIME: 15 minutes

15 ml lemon juice
15 ml olive oil
1 tsp. minced garlic
½ tsp. chilli powder
4 (170 g) tilapia fillets

1. In a large, shallow bowl, mix together the lemon juice, olive oil, garlic, and chilli powder to make a marinade. Place the tilapia fillets in the bowl and coat evenly.
2. Preheat the airfryer baskets with the grill plates inserted for three minutes by activating the automatic preheat key.
3. Carefully place 2 tilapia fillets in a single layer in each basket. Select the Match Cook key and set basket 1 to 180°C for 15 minutes and touch the start key to activate. Halfway through cooking, flip the tilapia fillets over.
4. When cooking is complete, transfer the tilapia fillets to a plate. Serve warm.

Sesame Seeds Coated Haddock

SERVES 4

| PREP TIME: 15 minutes
| COOK TIME: 18 minutes

45 ml olive oil
32 g plain flour
2 eggs
50 g sesame seeds, toasted
4 (170 g) frozen haddock fillets
50 g breadcrumbs
⅛ tsp. dried rosemary, crushed
Salt and ground black pepper, as required

1. Place the flour in a shallow bowl and whisk the eggs in a second bowl.
2. Mix the sesame seeds, breadcrumbs, rosemary, salt, black pepper and olive oil in a third bowl until a crumbly mixture is formed.
3. Coat each fillet with flour, dip into whisked eggs and finally, then dredge into the breadcrumb mixture.
4. Preheat the airfryer baskets with the grill plates inserted for three minutes by activating the automatic preheat key.
5. Carefully place 2 haddock fillets into each basket. Select the Match Cook key and set basket 1 to 180°C for 18 minutes and touch the start key to activate. Halfway through cooking, flip the haddock fillets over.
6. When cooking is complete, transfer the haddock fillets to a plate. Serve warm.

Orange Glazed Halibut Steak

SERVES 4

| PREP TIME: 30 minutes
| COOK TIME: 15 minutes

cooking spray
450 g halibut steaks
1 garlic clove, minced
¼ tsp. fresh ginger, grated finely
120 ml low-sodium soy sauce
60 ml fresh orange juice
30 ml lime juice
120 ml cooking wine
40 g sugar
¼ tsp. red pepper flakes, crushed

1. Put all the ingredients except halibut steaks in a pan and bring to a boil.
2. Cook for about 4 minutes, stirring continuously and remove from the heat.
3. Put the halibut steaks and half of the marinade in a resealable bag and shake well.
4. Refrigerate for about 1 hour and reserve the remaining marinade.
5. Preheat the airfryer baskets with the grill plates inserted for three minutes by activating the automatic preheat key.
6. Spray the grill plates with cooking spray. Place half of the halibut steaks in a single layer in each basket. Select the Match Cook key and set basket 1 to 180°C for 15 minutes and touch the start key to activate. Halfway through cooking, flip the halibut steaks over.
7. When cooking is complete, transfer the halibut steaks to a plate. Coat with the remaining glaze and serve hot.

Flavored Spring Rolls

SERVES 4

| PREP TIME: 10 minutes
| COOK TIME: 18 minutes

Cooking spray
240 g finely sliced cabbage
110 g matchstick cut carrots
2 (110 g) tins tiny prawns, drained
20 ml soy sauce
2 tsps. minced garlic
Salt and freshly ground black pepper, to taste
16 square spring roll wrappers

1. Spray a medium sauté pan with cooking spray.
2. Add the garlic to the sauté pan and cook over medium heat until fragrant, about 30 to 45 seconds. Add the cabbage and carrots and sauté until the vegetables are slightly tender, about 5 minutes.
3. Add the tiny prawns and soy sauce and season with salt and pepper to taste, then stir to combine well. Sauté until the moisture has evaporated, another 2 minutes. Set aside to cool.
4. Place a spring roll wrapper on a work surface so it looks like a diamond. Place 1 tbsp. of the prawn mixture on the lower end of the wrapper.
5. Roll the wrapper away from you halfway, then fold in the right and left sides, like an envelope. Continue to roll to the very end, using a little water to seal the edge. Repeat with the remaining wrappers and filling.
6. Preheat the airfryer baskets with the grill plates inserted for three minutes by activating the automatic preheat key.
7. Place half of spring rolls in a single layer in each basket. Lightly spray with cooking spray. Select the Match Cook key and set basket 1 to 190°C for 10 minutes and touch the start key to activate.
8. When cooking is complete, transfer the spring rolls to a plate. Let cool for 5 minutes before serving.

Zesty Mahi Mahi

SERVES 3

| PREP TIME: 10 minutes
| COOK TIME: 18 minutes

680 g Mahi Mahi fillets
1 lemon, cut into slices
3 g fresh dill, chopped
½ tsp. red chilli powder
Salt and ground black pepper, as required

1. Season the Mahi Mahi fillets evenly with chilli powder, salt and black pepper to taste.
2. Preheat the airfryer baskets with the grill plates inserted for three minutes by activating the automatic preheat key.
3. Carefully place half of the Mahi Mahi fillets in a single layer in each basket. Top with the lemon slices. Select the Match Cook key and set basket 1 to 180°C for 18 minutes and touch the start key to activate. Halfway through cooking, flip the Mahi Mahi fillets over.
4. When cooking is complete, transfer the lemon slices to a plate. Place the lemon slices over the Mahi Mahi. Garnish with fresh dill and serve warm.

CHAPTER 3

Vegetable

Honey Glazed Carrots

SERVES 4

| PREP TIME: 10 minutes
| COOK TIME: 16 minutes

400 g carrots, peeled and cut into large chunks
15 ml olive oil
15 ml honey
Salt and black pepper, to taste

1. Mix all the ingredients in a bowl and toss to coat well.
2. When ready to cook, remove the grill plate from basket 1 then preheat the airfryer basket for three minutes by activating the automatic preheat key.
3. Put the carrots into basket 1 and set the temperature to 200°C for 16 minutes then touch the start key to activate the airfryer. Halfway through cooking, flip the carrots over.
4. When cooking is complete, transfer carrots to a plate. Serve warm.

Roasted Green Beans

SERVES 3

| PREP TIME: 15 minutes
| COOK TIME: 12 minutes

5 g unsalted butter, melted
450 g green beans, trimmed and halved
15 ml fresh lemon juice
¼ tsp. garlic powder

1. Mix all the ingredients in a bowl and toss to coat well.
2. When ready to cook, remove the grill plate from basket 1 then preheat the airfryer basket for three minutes by activating the automatic preheat key.
3. Put the green beans into basket 1 and set the temperature to 200°C for 12 minutes then touch the start key to activate the airfryer. Halfway through cooking, carefully flip the green beans over.
4. Carefully remove the green beans from the airfryer using a silicone spatula. Serve warm.

Roasted Broccoli with Butter

SERVES 4

| PREP TIME: 10 minutes
| COOK TIME: 10 minutes

480 g fresh broccoli florets
30 g butter, melted
salt and black pepper, to taste

1. Mix the broccoli, butter, salt, and black pepper in a bowl and toss to coat well.
2. When ready to cook, remove the grill plate from basket 1 then preheat the airfryer basket for three minutes by activating the automatic preheat key.
3. Put the broccoli florets into basket 1 and set the temperature to 200°C for 10 minutes then touch the start key to activate the airfryer. Halfway through cooking, carefully flip the broccoli florets over.
4. Carefully remove the broccoli florets from the airfryer using a silicone spatula. Serve warm.

Hasselback Potatoes

SERVES 4

| PREP TIME: 20 minutes
| COOK TIME: 30 minutes

30 ml olive oil
4 potatoes
20 g Parmesan cheese, shredded
3 g fresh chives, chopped

1. Cut slits along each potato about 0.5 cm apart using a sharp knife, making sure slices should stay connected at the bottom.
2. Preheat the basket 1 with the grill plate inserted for three minutes by activating the automatic preheat key.
3. Coat the potatoes with olive oil and arrange in basket 1 and set the temperature to 200°C for 30 minutes then touch the start key to activate the airfryer.
4. When the potatoes are ready, transfer to a plate. Top with chives and Parmesan cheese to serve.

Perfectly Roasted Mushrooms

SERVES 4

| PREP TIME: 10 minutes
| COOK TIME: 25 minutes

900 g mushrooms, quartered
30 ml white vermouth
15 g butter, melted
2 g herbs de Provence
½ tsp. garlic powder

1. Mix the herbs de Provence, garlic powder and butter and mushrooms in a large bowl.
2. When ready to cook, remove the grill plates and preheat the airfryer baskets for three minutes by activating the automatic preheat key.
3. Place half of the mushrooms in a single layer in each basket. Select the Match Cook key then set basket 1 to 200°C for 25 minutes, then touch the start key to activate the airfryer.
4. When the mushrooms have been cooking for 20 minutes, stir the mushrooms with white vermouth and cook for a further 5 minutes until the mushrooms are fragrant.
5. When cooking is complete, transfer the mushrooms to a plate. Serve warm.

Simple Green Beans and Mushroom

SERVES 6

| PREP TIME: 15 minutes
| COOK TIME: 15 minutes

45 ml olive oil
670 g fresh green beans, trimmed
200 g fresh button mushrooms, sliced
40 g French fried onions
30 ml fresh lemon juice
1 tsp. ground sage
1 tsp. onion powder
1 tsp. garlic powder
Salt and black pepper, to taste

1. Mix the green beans, mushrooms, oil, lemon juice, sage, and spices in a bowl and toss to coat well.
2. Remove the grill plates from both baskets then preheat the airfryer baskets for three minutes by activating the automatic preheat key.
3. Transfer the green beans to basket 1, set the temperature to 200°C for 15 minutes; next add the mushrooms to basket 2 set the temperature to 200°C for 12 minutes. Select the Smart Finish key then touch the start key to activate the airfryer. Give both baskets a stir halfway through cooking.
4. When the green beans and mushrooms are ready, remove from the airfryer baskets using a silicone spoon. Serve warm.

Ultra-Crispy Tofu

SERVES 4

| PREP TIME: 15 minutes
| COOK TIME: 14 minutes

cooking spray
30 ml low-sodium soy sauce
30 ml fish sauce
340 g extra-firm tofu, drained and cubed into 2.5 cm size
5 g butter
5 ml sesame oil
1 tsp. chicken bouillon granules

1. Mix the soy sauce, fish sauce, sesame oil and chicken granules in a bowl and toss to coat well.
2. Stir in the tofu cubes and mix until well combined. Keep aside to marinate for about 30 minutes.
3. When ready to cook, remove the grill plate from basket 1 then preheat the airfryer basket for three minutes by activating the automatic preheat key.
4. Spray the tofu cubes with cooking spray and place into basket 1 and set the temperature to 200°C for 14 minutes then touch the start key to activate the airfryer. Halfway through cooking, flip the tofu cubes over.
5. When cooking is complete, transfer the tofu cubes to a plate. Serve warm.

Chewy Glazed Parsnips

SERVES 6

| PREP TIME: 10 minutes
| COOK TIME: 35 minutes

900 g parsnips, peeled and cut into 2.5-cm chunks
30 ml maple syrup
15 g butter, melted
1 tbsp. dried parsley flakes, crushed
¼ tsp. red pepper flakes, crushed

1. Mix the parsnips and butter in a bowl and toss to coat well.
2. When ready to cook, remove the grill plates and preheat the airfryer baskets for three minutes by activating the automatic preheat key.
3. Place half of the parsnips in each basket. Select the Match Cook key then set basket 1 to 200°C for 35 minutes, then touch the start key to activate the airfryer. Halfway through cooking, give the parsnips a shake.
4. Meanwhile, mix the remaining ingredients in a large bowl.
5. When the parsnips have been cooking for 30 minutes, spread the mixture over parsnips and cook for a further 5 minutes.
6. When cooking is complete, transfer the parsnips to a plate. Serve warm.

Indian Okra with Green Beans

SERVES 2

| PREP TIME: 10 minutes
| COOK TIME: 18 minutes

225 g frozen cut okra
225 g bag frozen cut green beans
30 g nutritional yeast
45 ml balsamic vinegar
Salt and black pepper, to taste

1. Mix the okra, green beans, vinegar, nutritional yeast, salt and black pepper in a bowl and toss to coat well.
2. When ready to cook, remove the grill plates and preheat the airfryer baskets for three minutes by activating the automatic preheat key.
3. Place half of the okra mixture in each basket. Select the Match Cook key then set basket 1 to 200°C for 18 minutes, then touch the start key to activate the airfryer. Halfway through cooking, give the okra mixture a shake.
4. When cooking is complete, transfer the okra mixture to a plate. Serve warm.

Garden Fresh Veggie Medley

SERVES 5

| PREP TIME: 10 minutes
| COOK TIME: 25 minutes

2 yellow bell peppers seeded and chopped
3 tomatoes, chopped
1 courgette, chopped
1 aubergine, chopped
2 small onions, chopped
15 ml olive oil
15 ml balsamic vinegar
2 garlic cloves, minced
10 g herbs de Provence
Salt and black pepper, to taste

1. Mix all the ingredients in a bowl and toss to coat well.
2. When ready to cook, remove the grill plates and preheat the airfryer baskets for three minutes by activating the automatic preheat key.
3. Place half of the vegetables in a single layer in each basket. Select the Match Cook key then set basket 1 to 200°C for 25 minutes, then touch the start key to activate the airfryer. Halfway through cooking, flip the vegetables over.
4. When cooking is complete, transfer the vegetables to a plate. Serve warm.

CHAPTER 4

Beef

Beef Meatballs

SERVES 5

| PREP TIME: 5 minutes
| COOK TIME: 16 minutes

450 g minced beef
60 g grated Parmesan cheese
50 g Mozzarella cheese
1 tbsp. minced garlic
1 tsp. freshly ground pepper

1. In a bowl, mix all the ingredients together in a large bowl.
2. Roll the meat mixture into 5 generous meatballs.
3. When ready to cook, remove the grill plate from basket 1 then pre-heat the airfryer basket for three minutes by activating the automatic preheat key.
4. Put the meatballs into basket 1 and set the temperature to 180°C for 16 minutes then touch the start key to activate the airfryer. Halfway through cooking, carefully flip the meatballs over.
5. When cooking is complete, transfer the meatballs to a plate. Serve warm.

Crispy Breaded Sirloin Steak

SERVES 2

| PREP TIME: 15 minutes
| COOK TIME: 18 minutes

120 g white flour
2 eggs
100 g panko breadcrumbs
2 (170 g) sirloin steaks, pounded
1 tsp. onion powder
1 tsp. garlic powder
Salt and black pepper, to taste

1. Place the flour in a shallow bowl and whisk the eggs in a second dish.
2. Mix the panko breadcrumbs and spices in a third bowl.
3. Rub the steaks with flour, then dip into the eggs and coat with breadcrumb mixture.
4. When ready to cook, remove the grill plate from basket 1 then pre-heat the airfryer basket for three minutes by activating the automatic preheat key.
5. Put the steaks into basket 1 and set the temperature to 180°C for 18 minutes then touch the start key to activate the airfryer. Halfway through cooking, carefully flip the steaks over.
6. When cooking is complete, transfer the steaks to a plate and cut into desired size slices to serve.

Beef Cheeseburgers

SERVES 2

| PREP TIME: 15 minutes
| COOK TIME: 13 minutes

225 g minced beef
10 g fresh coriander, minced
2 slices cheddar cheese
2 salad leaves
2 burger buns, cut into half
1 garlic clove, minced
Salt and black pepper, to taste

1. Mix the beef, garlic, coriander, salt, and black pepper in a bowl.
2. Make 2 equal-sized patties from the beef mixture.
3. Preheat the basket 1 with the grill plate inserted for three minutes by activating the automatic preheat key.
4. Carefully place patties into basket 1 and set the temperature to 180°C for 13 minutes then touch the start key to activate the airfryer.
5. When the chicken has been cooking for 12 minutes, top each patty with 1 cheese slice and cook for a further 1 minute until the cheese is melted.
6. When cooking is complete, transfer the patties to a plate. Place burger buns in a serving platter and arrange salad leaf between each bun. Top with 1 patty and immediately serve.

Bacon Wrapped Filet Mignon

SERVES 2

| PREP TIME: 15 minutes
| COOK TIME: 15 minutes

5 ml avocado oil
2 rashers of bacon
2 (170 g) filet mignon steaks
salt and black pepper, to taste

1. Wrap each mignon steak with 1 rasher of bacon and secure with a toothpick.
2. Season the steak generously with salt and black pepper and coat with avocado oil.
3. Preheat the basket 1 with the grill plate inserted for three minutes by activating the automatic preheat key.
4. Carefully place the steaks into basket 1 and set the temperature to 190°C for 15 minutes then touch the start key to activate the airfryer. Halfway through cooking, carefully flip the steaks over.
5. When cooking is complete, transfer the steaks to a plate and cut into desired size slices to serve.

Ribeye Steaks with Rosemary

SERVES 2

| PREP TIME: 10 minutes
| COOK TIME: 12 minutes

30 g butter
1 clove garlic, minced
20 ml balsamic vinegar
5 g rosemary, chopped
2 ribeye steaks
salt and ground black pepper, to taste

1. Melt the butter in a frying pan over medium heat. Add the garlic and fry until fragrant.
2. Remove the frying pan from the heat and add the salt, pepper, and vinegar. Allow it to cool.
3. Add the rosemary, then pour the mixture into a Ziploc bag.
4. Put the ribeye steaks in the bag and shake well, coating the meat well. Refrigerate for an hour, then allow to sit for a further 20 minutes.
5. Preheat the basket 1 with the grill plate inserted for three minutes by activating the automatic preheat key.
6. Carefully place the ribeyes into basket 1 and set the temperature to 180°C for 12 minutes then touch the start key to activate the airfryer. Halfway through cooking, carefully flip the ribeyes over.
7. When cooking is complete, transfer the ribeyes to a plate. Serve warm.

Beef Braising Steak with Brussels Sprouts

SERVES 4

| PREP TIME: 20 minutes
| COOK TIME: 25 minutes

450 g beef braising steak
30 ml vegetable oil
15 ml red wine vinegar
1 tsp. onion powder
1 tsp. smoked paprika
½ tsp. garlic powder
1 tsp. fine sea salt
½ tsp. ground black pepper
225 g Brussels sprouts, cleaned and halved
½ tsp. fennel seeds
1 tsp. dried sage
1 tsp. dried basil

1. Massage the beef with the vegetable oil, wine vinegar, salt, black pepper, paprika, onion powder, and garlic powder, coating it well. Let marinate for a minimum of 3 hours.
2. When ready to cook, remove the grill plate from basket 2 then preheat the airfryer baskets for three minutes by activating the automatic preheat key.
3. Remove the beef from the marinade and put onto the grill plate in basket 1 and set the temperature to 180°C for 20 minutes. Put the Brussels sprouts into basket 2 and set the temperature to 200°C for 25 minutes then activate the Smart Finish key and touch the start key to activate the airfryer. Halfway through cooking, turn the beef over and give the Brussels sprouts a shake.
4. When cooking is complete, serve the beef with Brussels sprouts.

Garlic Flank Steak

SERVES 4

| PREP TIME: 10 minutes
| COOK TIME: 12 minutes

450 g flank steaks, sliced
30 g xanthum gum
120 ml soy sauce
10 ml vegetable oil
140 g sugar, packed
½ tsp. ginger
1 tbsp. garlic, minced
120 ml water

1. Coat the steaks with xanthum gum on both the sides.
2. Preheat the basket 1 with the grill plate inserted for three minutes by activating the automatic preheat key.
3. Carefully place steaks into basket 1 and set the temperature to 180°C for 12 minutes then touch the start key to activate the airfryer. Halfway through cooking, carefully flip the steak slices over.
4. When cooking is complete, transfer the steak slices to a plate.
5. Meanwhile, cook rest of the ingredients for the sauce in a saucepan. Bring to a boil and pour over the steak slices to serve.

Beef Meatballs with Tomato Sauce

SERVES 8

| PREP TIME: 10 minutes
| COOK TIME: 15 minutes

450 g minced beef
1 egg, beaten
2 carrots, shredded
2 whole wheat bread slices, crumbled
1 small onion, minced
½ tsp. garlic salt
black pepper and salt, to taste
480 ml pasta sauce
240 ml tomato sauce

1. In a bowl, combine the minced beef, egg, carrots, crumbled bread, onion, garlic salt, black pepper and salt.
2. Divide the mixture into equal amounts and shape each one into a small meatball.
3. When ready to cook, remove the grill plate from basket 1 then preheat the airfryer basket for three minutes by activating the automatic preheat key.
4. Put the meatballs into basket 1 and set the temperature to 180°C for 10 minutes then touch the start key to activate the airfryer.
5. When cooking is complete, transfer the meatballs to an oven-safe dish and top with the tomato sauce and pasta sauce.
6. Set the dish into the basket 1 and cook at 160°C for 5 more minutes. Serve hot.

Steak with Bell Peppers

SERVES 4

| PREP TIME: 20 minutes
| COOK TIME: 18 minutes

570 g beef steak, cut into thin strips
2 green bell peppers, seeded and cubed
1 red bell pepper, seeded and cubed
1 red onion, sliced
1 tsp. dried oregano, crushed
1 tsp. onion powder
1 tsp. garlic powder
1 tsp. red chilli powder
1 tsp. paprika
Salt, to taste
30 ml olive oil

1. Mix the oregano and spices in a bowl.
2. Add the bell peppers, onion, oil, and beef strips and mix until well combined.
3. Remove the grill plates from both baskets then preheat the airfryer baskets for three minutes by activating the automatic preheat key.
4. Transfer the beef strips to basket 1, set the temperature to 200°C for 18 minutes; next add the vegetables to basket 2 set the temperature to 200°C for 15 minutes. Select the Smart Finish key then touch the start key to activate the airfryer. Give both baskets a stir halfway through cooking.
5. When the beef strips and vegetables are ready, remove from the airfryer baskets using a silicone spoon. Serve the beef strips hot with vegetables.

Air Fried Beef Ribs

SERVES 4

| PREP TIME: 20 minutes
| COOK TIME: 16 minutes

120 ml vegetable oil
45 ml apple cider vinegar
450 g meaty beef ribs, rinsed and drained
50 g coriander, finely chopped
2 garlic cloves, finely chopped
5 g fresh basil leaves, chopped
1 tsp. chipotle powder
1 tsp. fennel seeds
1 tsp. hot paprika
coarse salt and black pepper, to taste

1. Coat the ribs with the remaining ingredients and refrigerate for at least 3 hours.
2. When ready to cook, remove the grill plate from basket 1 then preheat the airfryer basket for three minutes by activating the automatic preheat key.
3. Separate the ribs from the marinade and put into basket 1 and set the temperature to 180°C for 16 minutes then touch the start key to activate the airfryer. Halfway through cooking, carefully flip the ribs over.
4. When cooking is complete, transfer the ribs to a plate. Pour the remaining marinade over the ribs before serving.

CHAPTER 5

Pork

Pork Chops with Rinds

SERVES 4

| PREP TIME: 5 minutes
| COOK TIME: 17 minutes

4 (110 g) pork chops
15 ml coconut oil, melted
1 tsp. chilli powder
½ tsp. garlic powder
45 g pork rinds, finely ground

1. Combine the chilli powder, garlic powder and ground pork rinds.
2. Coat the pork chops with coconut oil, followed by the pork rind mixture, taking care to cover them completely.
3. Preheat the airfryer baskets with the grill plates inserted for three minutes by activating the automatic preheat key.
4. Carefully place two pork chops into each basket. Select the Match Cook key and set basket 1 to 190°C for 17 minutes and touch the start key to activate. Halfway through cooking, flip the pork chops over.
5. When cooking is complete, transfer the pork chops to a plate. Serve warm.

Bacon Wrapped Pork Tenderloin with Apple Gravy

SERVES 4

| PREP TIME: 10 minutes
| COOK TIME: 20 minutes

For the Pork:
1 pork tenderloin
3 rashers of bacon
15 g Dijon mustard

For the Apple Gravy:
2 apples
45 ml ghee, divided
1 small shallot, chopped
8 g almond flour
240 ml vegetable broth
½ tsp. Dijon mustard

1. Spread the Dijon mustard all over the pork tenderloin and wrap with rashers of bacon.
2. Preheat the basket 1 with the grill plate inserted for three minutes by activating the automatic preheat key.
3. Carefully place the wrapped pork into basket 1 and set the temperature to 190°C for 20 minutes then touch the start key to activate the airfryer. Halfway through cooking, flip the pork over.
4. Meanwhile, heat 15 ml ghee in a pan and add shallots. Cook for 1 minute, then add the apples, cooking for 4 minutes until softened.
5. Add the flour and remaining 30 ml ghee to make a roux. Add the broth and mustard, stirring to combine well.
6. When sauce starts to bubble, add 240 g of sautéed apples, cooking until sauce thickens.
7. Once the pork tenderloin is cooked, let cool for 10 minutes to rest before slicing.
8. Serve topped with apple gravy.

Simple Pulled Pork

SERVES 1

| PREP TIME: 5 minutes
| COOK TIME: 22 minutes

5 g butter
25 g barbecue dry rub
450 g pork tenderloin
80 ml double cream

1. Massage the dry rub into the pork tenderloin, coating it well.
2. When ready to cook, remove the grill plate from basket 1 then pre-heat the airfryer basket for three minutes by activating the automatic preheat key.
3. Put the tenderloin into basket 1 and set the temperature to 190°C for 22 minutes then touch the start key to activate the airfryer.
4. When the pork has been cooking for 17 minutes, shred with two forks. Add the double cream and butter into the basket along with the shredded pork. Cook for a further 5 minutes until the cream and butter are melted and bubbling.
5. When cooking is complete, transfer the shredded pork to a plate. Allow to cool, then serve.

Cheese Ham Rolls

SERVES 4

| PREP TIME: 15 minutes
| COOK TIME: 15 minutes

340 g refrigerated pizza crust, rolled into 0.5-cm thickness
150 g cooked ham, sliced
320 g Cheddar cheese, shredded
90 g Mozzarella cheese, shredded
90 g roasted red bell peppers
15 ml olive oil

1. Arrange the ham, cheeses and roasted peppers over one side of dough and fold to seal.
2. Brush the dough evenly with olive oil.
3. When ready to cook, remove the grill plate from basket 1 then pre-heat the airfryer basket for three minutes by activating the automatic preheat key.
4. Put the dough into basket 1 and set the temperature to 180°C for 15 minutes then touch the start key to activate the airfryer. Halfway through cooking, carefully flip the dough over.
5. When cooking is complete, transfer the dough to a plate. Serve warm.

Pork Tenderloin with Bell Peppers

SERVES 3

| PREP TIME: 20 minutes
| COOK TIME: 22 minutes

310 g pork tenderloin, cut into 4 pieces
1 large red bell pepper, seeded and cut into thin strips
1 red onion, thinly sliced
15 ml olive oil
2 tsps. Herbs de Provence
½ tbsp. Dijon mustard
Salt and ground black pepper, as required

1. Mix the bell pepper, onion, Herbs de Provence, salt, black pepper and 7 ml oil in a bowl.
2. Rub the pork tenderloin evenly with mustard, salt, and black pepper and drizzle with the remaining oil.
3. When ready to cook, remove the grill plate from basket 2 then preheat the airfryer baskets for three minutes by activating the automatic preheat key.
4. Place the pork tenderloin onto the grill plate in basket 1 and set the temperature to 190°C for 22 minutes. Put the bell pepper mixture into basket 2 and set the temperature to 200°C for 15 minutes then activate the Smart Finish key and touch the start key to activate the airfryer. Halfway through cooking, carefully flip the tenderloin and bell pepper mixture over.
5. When cooking is complete, dish out the tenderloin and cut into desired size slices. Serve with bell pepper mixture.

BBQ Pork Steaks

SERVES 4

| PREP TIME: 5 minutes
| COOK TIME: 17 minutes

4 pork steaks
14 g Cajun seasoning
30 ml BBQ sauce
15 ml vinegar
5 ml soy sauce
100 g brown sugar
120 ml ketchup

1. Sprinkle the pork steaks with Cajun seasoning.
2. Combine the remaining ingredients and rub onto steaks.
3. Preheat the airfryer baskets with the grill plates inserted for three minutes by activating the automatic preheat key.
4. Place 2 steaks in a single layer in each basket. Select the Match Cook key and set basket 1 to 190°C for 17 minutes and touch the start key to activate. Halfway through cooking, carefully flip the steaks over.
5. When cooking is complete, transfer the steaks to a plate. Serve warm.

Pork Spare Ribs

SERVES 6

| PREP TIME: 15 minutes
| COOK TIME: 22 minutes

12 (2.5-cm) pork spare ribs
60 g cornflour
5-6 garlic cloves, minced
120 ml rice vinegar
30 ml soy sauce
30 ml olive oil
Salt and black pepper, to taste

1. Mix the garlic, vinegar, soy sauce, salt, and black pepper in a large bowl.
2. Coat the ribs generously with the mixture and refrigerate to marinate overnight.
3. Place the cornflour in a shallow bowl and dredge the ribs in it. Drizzle lightly with olive oil.
4. Preheat the airfryer baskets with the grill plates inserted for three minutes by activating the automatic preheat key.
5. Place half of ribs in a single layer in each basket. Select the Match Cook key and set basket 1 to 190°C for 22 minutes and touch the start key to activate. Halfway through cooking, carefully flip the ribs over.
6. When cooking is complete, transfer the ribs to a plate. Serve warm.

Pork with Aloha Salsa

SERVES 4

| PREP TIME: 20 minutes
| COOK TIME: 14 minutes

2 eggs
450 g boneless, thin pork cutlets (9-12mm thick)
30 ml milk
30 g flour
30 g panko bread crumbs
12 g sesame seeds
30 g cornflour
Cooking spray
Lemon pepper and salt, to taste
For the Aloha Salsa:
160 g fresh pineapple, chopped in small pieces
30 g green or red bell pepper, chopped
30 g red onion, finely chopped
5 ml low-sodium soy sauce
½ tsp. ground cinnamon
⅛ tsp. crushed red pepper
⅛ tsp. ground black pepper

1. In a medium bowl, stir together all ingredients for salsa. Cover and refrigerate while cooking the pork.
2. Beat the eggs and milk in a shallow dish.
3. In another shallow dish, mix the flour, panko bread crumbs, and sesame seeds.
4. Sprinkle the pork cutlets with lemon pepper and salt.
5. Dip the pork cutlets in cornflour, egg mixture, and then panko coating. Spray both sides with cooking spray.
6. Preheat the basket 1 with the grill plate inserted for three minutes by activating the automatic preheat key.
7. Carefully place the pork cutlets into basket 1 and set the temperature to 190°C for 14 minutes then touch the start key to activate the airfryer. Halfway through cooking, flip the pork cutlets over.
8. When cooking is complete, transfer the pork cutlets to a plate. Serve the fried cutlets with salsa on the side.

Cheesy Sausage Balls

SERVES 6

| PREP TIME: 5 minutes
| COOK TIME: 15 minutes

340 g pork sausage
170 g shredded Cheddar cheese
12 Cheddar cubes

1. Mix the shredded cheese and sausage.
2. Divide the mixture into 12 equal parts to be stuffed.
3. Add a cube of cheese to the centre of the sausage and roll into balls.
4. When ready to cook, remove the grill plates and preheat the airfryer baskets for three minutes by activating the automatic preheat key.
5. Place half of balls in a single layer in each basket. Select the Match Cook key then set basket 1 to 200°C for 15 minutes, then touch the start key to activate the airfryer. Halfway through cooking, carefully flip the balls over.
6. When cooking is complete, transfer the balls to a plate. Serve warm.

Pork Chops with Peanut Sauce

SERVES 4

| PREP TIME: 30 minutes
| COOK TIME: 15 minutes

For the Pork:
450 g pork chops, cubed into 2.5 cm size
1 garlic clove, minced
30 ml soy sauce
15 ml olive oil
5 ml hot pepper sauce
1 tsp. fresh ginger, minced
For the Peanut Sauce:
30 ml olive oil, divided
100 g ground peanuts
180 ml coconut milk
1 shallot, chopped finely
1 garlic clove, minced
1 tsp. ground coriander
5 ml hot pepper sauce

1. Mix all the pork ingredients in a bowl and keep aside for about 30 minutes.
2. When ready to cook, remove the grill plate from basket 1 then preheat the airfryer basket for three minutes by activating the automatic preheat key.
3. Put the pork into basket 1 and set the temperature to 190°C for 15 minutes then touch the start key to activate the airfryer. Halfway through cooking, carefully give the pork a shake.
4. Meanwhile, heat 15 ml olive oil in a pan on medium heat and add the shallot and garlic. Sauté for 3 minutes and stir in coriander. Sauté for about 1 minute and add the rest of the ingredients. Cook for about 5 minutes.
5. When cooking is complete, transfer the pork to a plate. Pour the peanut sauce over the pork to serve.

CHAPTER 6

Lamb

Roasted Lamb Leg

SERVES 4

| PREP TIME: 15 minutes
| COOK TIME: 1 hour

15 ml olive oil
1.1 kg half lamb leg roast, slits carved
2 garlic cloves, sliced into smaller slithers
1 tbsp. dried rosemary
Cracked Himalayan rock salt and cracked peppercorns, to taste

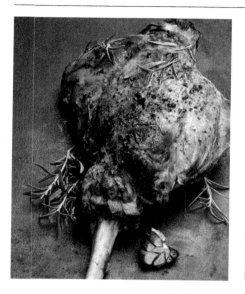

1. Insert the garlic slithers in the slits and brush with rosemary, oil, salt and black pepper to taste.
2. Preheat the basket 1 with the grill plate inserted for three minutes by activating the automatic preheat key.
3. Carefully place the lamb into basket 1 and set the temperature to 200°C for 1 hour then touch the start key to activate the airfryer. Halfway through cooking, flip the lamb over.
4. When the the lamb is ready, carefully remove from the airfryer with a silicone spatula, allow it to rest for a couple of minutes. Serve warm.

Nut Crusted Rack of Lamb

SERVES 6

| PREP TIME: 15 minutes
| COOK TIME: 35 minutes

800 g rack of lamb
1 egg
6 g breadcrumbs
85 g almonds, chopped finely
2 g fresh rosemary, chopped
15 ml olive oil
1 garlic clove, minced
salt and black pepper, to taste

1. Mix the garlic, olive oil, salt and black pepper in a bowl.
2. Whisk the egg in a shallow dish and mix the breadcrumbs, almonds and rosemary in another shallow dish.
3. Coat the rack of lamb with garlic mixture evenly, dip into the egg and then dredge into the breadcrumb mixture.
4. Preheat the basket 1 with the grill plate inserted for three minutes by activating the automatic preheat key.
5. Carefully place the rack of lamb into basket 1 and set the temperature to 200°C for 35 minutes then touch the start key to activate the airfryer. Halfway through cooking, flip the rack of lamb over.
6. When cooking is complete, transfer the rack of lamb to a plate. Serve warm.

Lamb Meatballs

SERVES 4

| PREP TIME: 20 minutes
| COOK TIME: 27 minutes

For the Meatballs:
450 g minced lamb
½ small onion, finely diced
1 clove garlic, minced
30 ml milk
1 egg yolk
5 g fresh parsley, finely chopped (plus more for garnish)
2 tsps. fresh oregano, finely chopped
salt and freshly ground black pepper, to taste

60 g crumbled feta cheese, for garnish
For the Tomato Sauce:
30 g butter
1 clove garlic, smashed
¼ tsp. ground cinnamon
1 (800 g) tain crushed tomatoes
Pinch crushed red pepper flakes
Salt, to taste
Cooking spray

1. Combine all the meatballs ingredients in a large bowl and mix just until everything is combined. Shape the mixture into 4-cm balls or shape the meat between two spoons to make quenelles.
2. Start the quick tomato sauce. Put the butter, garlic and red pepper flakes in a sauté pan and heat over medium heat on the hob. Let the garlic sizzle a little, but before the butter browns, add the cinnamon and tomatoes. Bring to a simmer and simmer for 15 minutes. Season with salt to taste.
3. When ready to cook, remove the grill plates and preheat the airfryer baskets for three minutes by activating the automatic preheat key.
4. Place half of the meatballs in a single layer in each basket. Select the Match Cook key then set basket 1 to 200°C for 12 minutes, then touch the start key to activate the airfryer. Halfway through cooking, flip the meatballs over.
5. When cooking is complete, transfer the meatballs to a plate. To serve, spoon a pool of the tomato sauce onto plates and put the meatballs. Sprinkle the feta cheese on top and garnish with more fresh parsley. Serve warm.

Simple Leg of Lamb with Brussels Sprouts

SERVES 6

| PREP TIME: 20 minutes
| COOK TIME: 1 hour

1 kg leg of lamb
680 g Brussels sprouts, trimmed
2 g fresh rosemary, minced
2 g fresh lemon thyme
45 ml olive oil, divided
30 ml honey
1 garlic clove, minced
salt and ground black pepper, as required

1. Make slits in the leg of lamb with a sharp knife.
2. Mix 30 ml olive oil, herbs, garlic, salt, and black pepper in a bowl.
3. Coat the leg of lamb with the oil mixture generously.
4. When ready to cook, remove the grill plate from basket 2 then preheat the airfryer baskets for three minutes by activating the automatic preheat key.
5. Place the leg of lamb onto the grill plate in basket 1 and set the temperature to 200°C for 1 hour. Coat the Brussels sprouts evenly with the remaining oil and honey and arrange in basket 2 and set the temperature to 200°C for 28 minutes then activate the Smart Finish key and touch the start key to activate the airfryer. Halfway through cooking carefully turn the leg of lamb and give the Brussels sprouts a shake.
6. When cooking is complete, serve the lamb with Brussels sprouts.

Spicy Lamb Kebabs

SERVES 6

| PREP TIME: 20 minutes
| COOK TIME: 8 minutes

Olive oil
4 eggs, beaten
150 g pistachios, chopped
450 g minced lamb
30 g plain flour
20 g flat-leaf parsley, chopped
2 tsps. chilli flakes
4 garlic cloves, minced

30 ml fresh lemon juice
2 tsps. cumin seeds
2 tsps. dried mint
1 tsp. fennel seeds
1 tsp. coriander seeds
2 tsps. salt
1 tsp. freshly ground black pepper

1. Mix the lamb, pistachios, eggs, lemon juice, chilli flakes, flour, fennel seeds, coriander seeds, cumin seeds, mint, parsley, salt and black pepper in a large bowl.
2. Thread the lamb mixture onto metal skewers to form sausages and coat with olive oil.
3. Preheat the basket 1 with the grill plate inserted for three minutes by activating the automatic preheat key.
4. Carefully place the skewers into basket 1 and set the temperature to 190°C for 8 minutes then touch the start key to activate the airfryer. Halfway through cooking, flip the skewers over.
5. When cooking is complete, transfer the skewers to a plate. Serve hot.

Simple Lamb Chops

SERVES 2

| PREP TIME: 10 minutes
| COOK TIME: 12 minutes

4 (115 g) lamb chops
Salt and black pepper, to taste
15 ml olive oil

1. Mix the olive oil, salt, and black pepper in a large bowl and add the lamb chops.
2. Preheat the basket 1 with the grill plate inserted for three minutes by activating the automatic preheat key.
3. Carefully place the chops into basket 1 and set the temperature to 180°C for 12 minutes then touch the start key to activate the airfryer. Halfway through cooking, flip the lamb chops over.
4. When the chops are ready, carefully transfer the chops to a plate with a silicone spatula. Serve warm.

Lamb Burger

SERVES 4

| PREP TIME: 15 minutes
| COOK TIME: 22-23 minutes

10 ml olive oil
450 g minced lamb
70 g black olives, finely chopped
40 g crumbled feta cheese
⅓ onion, finely chopped
1 clove garlic, minced
8 g fresh parsley, finely chopped
1½ tsps. fresh oregano, finely chopped
½ tsp. salt
freshly ground black pepper
4 thick pitta breads
toppings and condiments

1. Preheat a medium frying pan over medium-high heat on the hob. Add the olive oil and cook the onion until tender, but not browned about 4 to 5 minutes. Add the garlic and cook for 1 minute. Transfer the onion and garlic to a mixing bowl and add the minced lamb, olives, feta cheese, parsley, oregano, salt and pepper. Gently mix the ingredients together.
2. Divide the mixture into 4 equal portions, then form the hamburgers, being careful not to over-handle the meat. One good way to do this is to throw the meat back and forth between the hands like a baseball, packing the meat each time you catch it. Flatten the balls into patties, making an indentation in the centre of each patty. Flatten the sides of the patties as well to make it easier to fit them into the basket.
3. Preheat the airfryer baskets with the grill plates inserted for three minutes by activating the automatic preheat key.
4. Place 2 burgers in a single layer in each basket. Select the Match Cook key and set basket 1 to 180°C for 16 minutes and touch the start key to activate. Halfway through cooking, flip the burgers over.
5. When cooking is complete, transfer the burgers to a plate and let the burgers rest for a few minutes before dressing and serving.
6. While the burgers are resting, bake the pitta breads at 180°C for 2 minutes. Tuck the burgers into the toasted pitta breads, or wrap the pittas around the burgers and serve with a tzatziki sauce or some mayonnaise.

Za'atar Lamb Loin Chops

SERVES 4

| PREP TIME: 10 minutes
| COOK TIME: 16 minutes

8 (100 g) bone-in lamb loin chops, trimmed
3 garlic cloves, crushed
15 ml fresh lemon juice
5 ml olive oil
1 tbsp. Za'atar
Salt and black pepper, to taste

1. Mix the garlic, lemon juice, oil, Za'atar, salt, and black pepper in a large bowl.
2. Coat the chops generously with the herb mixture.
3. Preheat the airfryer baskets with the grill plates inserted for three minutes by activating the automatic preheat key.
4. Carefully place 4 chops in a single layer into each basket. Select the Match Cook key and set basket 1 to 200°C for 16 minutes and touch the start key to activate. Halfway through cooking, flip the chops over.
5. When cooking is complete, transfer the chops to a plate. Serve warm.

(Note: Za'atar - Za'atar is generally made with ground dried thyme, oregano, marjoram, or some combination thereof, mixed with toasted sesame seeds, and salt, though other spices such as sumac might also be added. Some commercial varieties also include roasted flour.)

Greek Lamb Pitta Pockets

SERVES 4

| PREP TIME: 15 minutes
| COOK TIME: 12 minutes

For the Dressing:
240 ml plain yoghurt
15 ml lemon juice
1 tsp. ground oregano
1 tsp. dried dill, crushed
½ tsp. salt
For the Meatballs:
225 g minced lamb
10 g diced onion
1 tsp. dried dill, crushed
1 tsp. dried parsley
¼ tsp. coriander
¼ tsp. oregano
¼ tsp. ground cumin
¼ tsp. salt
4 pitta halves
Suggested Toppings:
1 medium cucumber, deseeded, thinly sliced
crumbled Feta cheese
1 red onion, slivered
chopped fresh peppers
sliced black olives

1. Stir all the dressing ingredients together in a small bowl and refrigerate while preparing lamb.
2. Combine all the meatball ingredients in a large bowl and stir to distribute seasonings.
3. Shape the meat mixture into 12 small meatballs, rounded or slightly flattened if you prefer.
4. When ready to cook, remove the grill plates and preheat the airfryer baskets for three minutes by activating the automatic preheat key.
5. Place half of the meatballs in a single layer in each basket. Select the Match Cook key then set basket 1 to 180°C for 12 minutes, then touch the start key to activate the airfryer. Halfway through cooking, carefully flip the meatballs over.
6. When cooking is complete, transfer the meatballs and drain on paper towels.
7. To serve, pile meatballs and the choice of toppings in the pitta pockets and drizzle with the dressing.

Roasted Lamb Chops with Avocado Mayo

SERVES 2

| PREP TIME: 5 minutes
| COOK TIME: 12 minutes

2 lamb chops
2 avocados
2 tsps. Italian herbs
120 ml mayonnaise
15 ml lemon juice

1. Season the lamb chops with the Italian herbs, then set aside for about 5 minutes.
2. Preheat the basket 1 with the grill plate inserted for three minutes by activating the automatic preheat key.
3. Carefully place the lamb chops into basket 1 and set the temperature to 180°C for 12 minutes then touch the start key to activate the airfryer. Halfway through cooking, flip the lamb chops over.
4. In the meantime, halve the avocados and open to remove the pits. Spoon the flesh into a blender.
5. Put the mayonnaise and lemon juice and pulse until a smooth consistency is achieved.
6. When cooking is complete, transfer the lamb chops to a plate. Serve warm with the avocado mayo.

CHAPTER 7

Wraps, Tacos and Sandwiches

Turkey, Hummus and Cheese Wraps

SERVES 4

| PREP TIME: 10 minutes
| COOK TIME: 8 minutes

120 ml hummus
4 large whole wheat wraps
16 thin slices deli turkey
40 g fresh baby spinach, or more to taste
8 slices Parmesan cheese

1. To assemble, place 2 tbsps. of hummus on each wrap and spread to within about 1-cm from edges. Top with 4 slices of turkey and 2 slices of Parmesan cheese. Finish with 10 g baby spinach, or pile on as much as you like.
2. Roll up each wrap. You don't need to fold or seal the ends.
3. When ready to cook, remove the grill plates and preheat the airfryer baskets for three minutes by activating the automatic preheat key.
4. Place 2 wraps in each basket. Select the Match Cook key then set basket 1 to 180°C for 8 minutes, then touch the start key to activate the airfryer.
5. When cooking is complete, transfer the wraps to a plate. Serve warm.

Cheesy Greens Sandwich

SERVES 4

| PREP TIME: 15 minutes
| COOK TIME: 8 minutes

Cooking spray
10 ml olive oil
90 g chopped mixed greens
2 garlic cloves, thinly sliced
2 slices low-sodium low-fat Emmental cheese
4 slices low-sodium whole-wheat bread

1. In a frying pan over medium heat, add the greens, garlic, and olive oil. Cook for about to 5 minutes, until the vegetables are tender. Drain, if necessary.
2. Make 2 sandwiches, dividing half of the greens and 1 slice of Emmental cheese between 2 slices of bread. Lightly spray the outsides of the sandwiches with cooking spray.
3. Preheat the basket 1 with the grill plate inserted for three minutes by activating the automatic preheat key.
4. Place the sandwiches into basket 1 and set the temperature to 200°C for 8 minutes then touch the start key to activate the airfryer. Halfway through cooking, flip the sandwiches over.
5. When cooking is complete, transfer the sandwiches to a plate. Cut each sandwich in half and serve.

Tuna and Lettuce Wraps

SERVES 4

| PREP TIME: 10 minutes
| COOK TIME: 10 minutes

cooking spray
450 g fresh tuna steak, cut into 2.5-cm cubes
6 g grated fresh ginger
2 garlic cloves, minced
2 ml toasted sesame oil
4 low-sodium whole-wheat tortillas
60 ml low-fat mayonnaise
120 g shredded romaine lettuce
1 red bell pepper, thinly sliced

1. In a medium bowl, mix the tuna, ginger, garlic, and sesame oil. Let it stand for 10 minutes.
2. When ready to cook, remove the grill plate from basket 1 then pre-heat the airfryer basket for three minutes by activating the automatic preheat key.
3. Spray the basket with cooking spray and place the tuna into basket 1 and set the temperature to 180°C for 10 minutes then touch the start key to activate the airfryer. Halfway through cooking, carefully give the tuna a shake.
4. When cooking is complete, carefully remove the tuna from the air-fryer using a silicone spatula.
5. Make the wraps with the tuna, tortillas, mayonnaise, lettuce, and bell pepper. Serve immediately.

Cajun-Style Fish Tacos with Lime

SERVES 6

| PREP TIME: 5 minutes
| COOK TIME: 18 minutes

10 ml avocado oil
1 tbsp. Cajun seasoning
4 tilapia fillets
1 (400 g) package coleslaw mix
12 corn tortillas
2 limes, cut into wedges

1. In a medium, shallow bowl, mix the avocado oil and the Cajun sea-soning to make a marinade. Add the tilapia fillets and coat evenly.
2. Preheat the airfryer baskets with the grill plates inserted for three minutes by activating the automatic preheat key.
3. Carefully place 2 tilapia fillets in a single layer in each basket. Select the Match Cook key and set basket 1 to 180°C for 18 minutes and touch the start key to activate. Halfway through cooking, flip the tilapia fillets over.
4. When cooking is complete, transfer the tilapia fillets to a plate. As-semble the tacos by placing some of the coleslaw mix in each torti-lla. Add ⅓ of a tilapia fillet to each tortilla. Squeeze some lime juice over the top of each taco and serve.

Smoky Chicken Sandwich

SERVES 2

| PREP TIME: 10 minutes
| COOK TIME: 20 minutes

Cooking spray
2 boneless, skinless chicken breasts (225 g each), sliced horizontally in half and separated into 4 thinner cutlets
50 g plain flour
3 large eggs, lightly beaten
120 ml marinara sauce
50 g dried bread crumbs
coarse salt and freshly ground black pepper, to taste
1 tbsp. smoked paprika
170 g smoked Mozzarella cheese, grated
2 store-bought soft, sesame-seed hamburger or Italian buns, split

1. Season the chicken cutlets all over with salt and pepper to taste.
2. Set up three shallow bowls: Place the flour in the first bowl, the eggs in the second and stir together the bread crumbs and smoked paprika in the third.
3. Coat the chicken pieces in the flour, then dip fully in the egg. Dredge in the paprika bread crumbs, then transfer to a wire rack set over a baking sheet and spray both sides liberally with cooking spray.
4. Preheat the airfryer baskets with the grill plates inserted for three minutes by activating the automatic preheat key.
5. Carefully place 2 chicken cutlets into each basket. Select the Match Cook key and set basket 1 to 180°C for 20 minutes and touch the start key to activate.
6. When the chicken has been cooking for 15 minutes, Spread each cutlet with 2 tbsps. of the marinara sauce and sprinkle with one-quarter of the smoked Mozzarella. Cook for a further 5 minutes until the chicken is cooked and the cheese is bubbling.
7. When cooking is complete, transfer the cutlets to a plate, stack on top of each other, and place 2 cutlets inside a bun. Serve the sandwiches warm.

Classic Cheese Sandwich

SERVES 2

| PREP TIME: 5 minutes
| COOK TIME: 8 minutes

30 ml mayonnaise
4 thick slices Brie cheese
4 thick slices sourdough bread
8 slices cured Italian meat

1. Spread the mayonnaise on one side of each slice of bread.
2. Preheat the basket 1 with the grill plate inserted for three minutes by activating the automatic preheat key.
3. Place 2 slices of bread into basket 1, mayonnaise-side down. Put the slices of Brie and cured Italian meat on the bread and cover with the remaining two slices of bread, mayonnaise-side up. Set the temperature to 180°C for 8 minutes then touch the start key to activate the airfryer. Halfway through cooking, flip the sandwiches over.
4. When cooking is complete, transfer the sandwiches to a plate. Serve immediately.

Red Cabbage and Fish Tacos

SERVES 4

| PREP TIME: 10 minutes
| COOK TIME: 10 minutes

450 g white fish fillets
10 ml olive oil
45 ml freshly squeezed lemon juice, divided
120 g chopped red cabbage
1 large carrot, grated
120 ml low-sodium salsa
80 ml low-fat Greek yoghurt
4 soft low-sodium whole-wheat tortillas

1. Brush the fish with the olive oil and sprinkle with 15 ml lemon juice.
2. Preheat the basket 1 with the grill plate inserted for three minutes by activating the automatic preheat key.
3. Place the fish into basket 1 and set the temperature to 200°C for 10 minutes then touch the start key to activate the airfryer. Halfway through cooking, flip the fish over.
4. Meanwhile, in a medium bowl, stir together the remaining 30 ml lemon juice, red cabbage, carrot, salsa and yoghurt.
5. When cooking is complete, transfer the fish to a plate and break it up into large pieces.
6. Offer the fish, tortillas and the cabbage mixture, and let each person assemble a taco. Serve warm.

Vegan Nugget and Pepper Taco Wraps

SERVES 4

| PREP TIME: 5 minutes
| COOK TIME: 14 minutes

15 ml water
4 pieces commercial vegan nuggets, chopped
1 small red bell pepper, chopped
1 small yellow onion, diced
2 cobs grilled corn kernels
4 large corn tortillas
Mixed greens, for garnish

1. Over a medium heat, sauté the nuggets in the water with the onion, corn kernels and bell pepper in a frying pan, then remove from the heat.
2. Fill the tortillas with the nuggets and vegetables and fold them up.
3. When ready to cook, remove the grill plates and preheat the airfryer baskets for three minutes by activating the automatic preheat key.
4. Place 2 tortillas in a single layer in each basket. Select the Match Cook key then set basket 1 to 180°C for 14 minutes, then touch the start key to activate the airfryer.
5. When cooking is complete, transfer the tortillas to a plate. Serve immediately, garnished with the mixed greens.

Cheesy Prawns Sandwich

SERVES 4

| PREP TIME: 10 minutes
| COOK TIME: 7 minutes

1 (170 g) tin tiny prawns, drained
150 g shredded Cheddar cheese
45 ml mayonnaise
12 g minced green onion
30 g softened butter
4 slices whole grain or whole-wheat bread

1. In a medium bowl, combine the prawns, mayonnaise, cheese and green onion, and mix well.
2. Spread this mixture on two of the slices of bread. Top with the other slices of bread to make two sandwiches. Spread the sandwiches lightly with butter.
3. Preheat the basket 1 with the grill plate inserted for three minutes by activating the automatic preheat key.
4. Place the sandwiches into basket 1 and set the temperature to 200°C for 7 minutes then touch the start key to activate the airfryer. Cook until the bread is browned and crisp and the cheese is melted.
5. When cooking is complete, transfer the sandwiches to a plate. Cut in half and serve warm.

Banana Egg Oatmeal Sandwich

SERVES 4

| PREP TIME: 5 minutes
| COOK TIME: 8 minutes

2 medium bananas, cut into 1-cm-thick slices
8 slices oat nut bread or any whole-grain, oversize bread
20 g cornflakes, crushed
20 g desiccated coconut
120 g pineapple preserves
90 g peanut butter
1 egg, beaten
Cooking spray

1. In a shallow dish, mix the cornflake crumbs and coconut and combine well.
2. For each sandwich, spread one bread slice with 22.5 g peanut butter. Top with banana slices. Spread another bread slice with 30 g preserves. Combine to make a sandwich.
3. Using a pastry brush, brush top of sandwich lightly with beaten egg. Sprinkle with about 5 g crumb coating, pressing it in to make it stick. Spray with cooking spray.
4. Turn the sandwich over and repeat to coat and spray the other side.
5. Preheat the airfryer baskets with the grill plates inserted for three minutes by activating the automatic preheat key.
6. Carefully place 2 sandwiches in a single layer in each basket. Select the Match Cook key and set basket 1 to 180°C for 8 minutes and touch the start key to activate. Halfway through cooking, flip the sandwiches over.
7. When cooking is complete, transfer the sandwiches to a plate. Cut the cooked sandwiches in half and serve warm.

CHAPTER 8

Poultry

Spicy Chicken Breasts

SERVES 4

| PREP TIME: 20 minutes
| COOK TIME: 30 minutes

cooking spray
30 g butter, melted
4 (170 g) boneless, skinless chicken breasts
¼ tsp. smoked paprika
¼ tsp. onion powder
¼ tsp. garlic powder
Salt and black pepper, as required

1. Mix the butter and spices in a bowl and coat the chicken with this mixture.
2. Preheat the airfryer baskets with the grill plates inserted for three minutes by activating the automatic preheat key.
3. Carefully place 2 chicken breasts in a single layer in each basket. Select the Match Cook key and set basket 1 to 180°C for 30 minutes and touch the start key to activate. Halfway through cooking, carefully flip the chicken breasts over.
4. When cooking is complete, transfer the chicken breasts to a plate. Serve warm.

Poussin Chicken

SERVES 4

| PREP TIME: 20 minutes
| COOK TIME: 30 minutes

60 ml olive oil
900 g poussin chicken, backbone removed and halved
4 g sugar
1 tsp. fresh rosemary, chopped
1 tsp. fresh thyme, chopped
1 tsp. fresh lemon zest, finely grated
¼ tsp. red pepper flakes, crushed
Salt and black pepper, to taste

1. Mix the olive oil, herbs, lemon zest, sugar, and spices in a bowl.
2. Stir in the poussin chicken and refrigerate to marinate for about 24 hours.
3. When ready to cook, remove the grill plate from basket 1 then preheat the airfryer basket for three minutes by activating the automatic preheat key.
4. Put the poussin chicken into basket 1 and set the temperature to 200°C for 30 minutes then touch the start key to activate the airfryer. Halfway through cooking, carefully turn the poussin chicken over.
5. When cooking is complete, transfer the poussin chicken to a plate. Serve hot.

Simple BBQ Chicken Wings

SERVES 4

| PREP TIME: 10 minutes
| COOK TIME: 25 minutes

900 g chicken wings, cut into drumettes and flats
120 ml BBQ sauce

1. Preheat the basket 1 with the grill plate inserted for three minutes by activating the automatic preheat key.
2. Place the chicken wings into basket 1 and set the temperature to 200°C for 25 minutes then touch the start key to activate the airfryer. Halfway through cooking, flip the chicken wings over.
3. When cooking is complete, transfer chicken wings to a plate. Drizzle with the BBQ sauce to serve.

Grilled Chicken and Veggie Kebabs

SERVES 3

| PREP TIME: 20 minutes
| COOK TIME: 25 minutes

450 g skinless, boneless chicken thighs, cut into cubes
2 small tomatoes, seeded and cut into large chunks
1 large red onion, cut into large chunks
120 ml plain Greek yoghurt
2 tsps. curry powder
15 ml olive oil
Wooden skewers, presoaked
½ tsp. smoked paprika
¼ tsp. cayenne pepper
Salt, to taste

1. Mix the chicken, olive oil, yoghurt and spices in a large baking dish.
2. Thread the chicken cubes, tomatoes and onion onto presoaked wooden skewers.
3. Coat the skewers generously with marinade and refrigerate for about 3 hours.
4. Preheat the airfryer baskets with the grill plates inserted for three minutes by activating the automatic preheat key.
5. Carefully place half of the skewers in each basket. Select the Match Cook key and set basket 1 to 180°C for 25 minutes and touch the start key to activate. Halfway through cooking, flip the skewers over.
6. When cooking is complete, transfer the skewers to a plate. Serve warm.

Crispy Herbed Turkey Breast

SERVES 2

| PREP TIME: 5 minutes
| COOK TIME: 30 minutes

2 turkey breasts
1 tbsp. ginger, minced
1 garlic clove, minced
½ tbsp. fresh parsley, chopped
½ tbsp. fresh rosemary, chopped
1 tsp. five spice powder
Salt and black pepper, to taste

1. Mix the garlic, herbs, five spice powder, salt and black pepper in a bowl.
2. Brush the turkey breasts generously with garlic mixture.
3. Preheat the basket 1 with the grill plate inserted for three minutes by activating the automatic preheat key.
4. Place the turkey breasts into basket 1 and set the temperature to 200°C for 30 minutes then touch the start key to activate the airfryer. Halfway through cooking, flip the turkey breasts over.
5. When cooking is complete, transfer the turkey breasts to a plate. Serve warm.

Spicy Chicken Legs

SERVES 3

| PREP TIME: 15 minutes
| COOK TIME: 22 minutes

15 ml olive oil
3 (225 g) chicken legs
240 ml buttermilk
220 g white flour
1 tsp. ground cumin
1 tsp. garlic powder
1 tsp. onion powder
1 tsp. paprika
Salt and ground black pepper, as required

1. Mix the chicken legs and buttermilk in a bowl and refrigerate for 2 hours.
2. Combine the flour and spices in another bowl and dredge the chicken legs into this mixture.
3. Now, dip the chicken into the buttermilk and coat again with the flour mixture.
4. When ready to cook, remove the grill plate from basket 1 then pre-heat the airfryer basket for three minutes by activating the automatic preheat key.
5. Put the chicken legs into basket 1 and drizzle with the oil. Set the temperature to 200°C for 22 minutes then touch the start key to activate the airfryer. Halfway through cooking, flip the chicken legs over.
6. When cooking is complete, transfer the chicken legs to a plate. Serve warm.

Sweet and Spicy Chicken Drumsticks

SERVES 4

| PREP TIME: 15 minutes
| COOK TIME: 20 minutes

4 (170 g) chicken drumsticks
1 garlic clove, crushed
15 ml mustard
15 ml vegetable oil
8 g brown sugar
1 tsp. cayenne pepper
1 tsp. red chilli powder
Salt and ground black pepper, as required

1. Mix the garlic, mustard, brown sugar, oil, and spices in a bowl.
2. Rub the chicken drumsticks with marinade and refrigerate for about 30 minutes.
3. When ready to cook, remove the grill plate from basket 1 then preheat the airfryer basket for three minutes by activating the automatic preheat key.
4. Put the drumsticks into basket 1 and set the temperature to 200°C for 20 minutes then touch the start key to activate the airfryer. Halfway through cooking, carefully flip the drumsticks over.
5. When cooking is complete, transfer the drumsticks to a plate. Serve warm.

Crispy Chicken Fillets with Coconut Rice

SERVES 4

| PREP TIME: 24 minutes
| COOK TIME: 30 minutes

4 (115 g) skinless, boneless chicken breasts
500 ml water
1 (400 ml) tin coconut milk
190 g rice
For the Marinade:
120 ml coconut cream
1 garlic clove, minced
1 tsp. fresh lime zest, grated finely
30 ml fresh lime juice
15 ml avocado oil

10 ml pure maple syrup
10 ml soy sauce
2 tsps. curry powder
1½ tsps. ground coriander
1 tsp. ground cumin
¼ tsp. dried coriander, crushed
¼ tsp. chile paste
Salt, to taste
Pinch of cayenne pepper

1. Put all the marinade ingredients in a large bowl and mix until well combined.
2. Stir in the chicken and coat generously with marinade.
3. Cover the bowl and refrigerate for about 24 hours.
4. Preheat the airfryer baskets with the grill plates inserted for three minutes by activating the automatic preheat key.
5. Carefully place 2 chicken breasts in a single layer into each basket. Select the Match Cook key and set basket 1 to 180°C for 30 minutes and touch the start key to activate. Halfway through cooking, flip the chicken breasts over.
6. Meanwhile, mix the water, coconut milk, rice and salt in a pan and bring to a boil. Lower the heat, cover and let it simmer for about 15 minutes.
7. When cooking is complete, transfer the chicken breasts to a plate. Serve chicken hot with coconut rice.

Traditional Mongolian Chicken

SERVES 4

| PREP TIME: 15 minutes
| COOK TIME: 20 minutes

450 g boneless chicken, cubed
1 egg
6 g cornflour
1 medium yellow onion, sliced thinly
120 ml evaporated milk
30 ml olive oil
15 ml light soy sauce
5 curry leaves

15 ml chilli sauce
3 tsps. garlic, minced
1 tsp. fresh ginger, grated
½ tsp. curry powder
5 g coconut sugar
½ tsp. salt
Pinch of black pepper

1. Mix the chicken, egg, soy sauce and cornflour in a bowl.
2. Cover and marinate for about 1 hour.
3. When ready to cook, remove the grill plate from basket 1 then preheat the airfryer basket for three minutes by activating the automatic preheat key.
4. Put the cubed chicken into basket 1 and set the temperature to 180°C for 14 minutes then touch the start key to activate the airfryer. Halfway through cooking, carefully give the chicken a shake.
5. When cooking is complete, transfer the chicken to a plate. Set aside.
6. Heat the olive oil in a frying pan on medium heat and add the onion, garlic and ginger.
7. Sauté for 2 minutes and stir in the chicken, curry powder, chilli sauce, sugar, salt and black pepper to taste.
8. Mix until well combined and whisk in evaporated milk.
9. Cook for about 4 minutes and dish out to serve warm.

Cheesy Chicken Breasts with Courgette

SERVES 2

| PREP TIME: 20 minutes
| COOK TIME: 30 minutes

2 (170 g) chicken breasts
1 egg, beaten
115 g breadcrumbs
30 ml vegetable oil
30 g grated Parmesan cheese, divided
3 g fresh basil
60 ml pasta sauce
15 ml olive oil, divided
1 small courgette, sliced into 1-cm thick rounds
2 tbsps. fat-free Italian dressing
Salt, to taste

1. Whisk the egg in a bowl and mix breadcrumbs, vegetable oil and basil in another bowl.
2. Dip the chicken breasts into the egg and then coat with the breadcrumb mixture.
3. Mix the courgette, 2 tbsps. Parmesan cheese, olive oil, Italian dressing, and salt in a medium bowl and toss to coat evenly.
4. When ready to cook, remove the grill plate from basket 2 then preheat the airfryer baskets for three minutes by activating the automatic preheat key.
5. Place the chicken breasts onto the grill plate in basket 1 and set the temperature to 180°C for 30 minutes. Put the courgette slices into basket 2 and set the temperature to 200°C for 20 minutes then activate the Smart Finish key and touch the start key to activate the airfryer.
6. When the chicken has been cooking for 20 minutes, top the chicken breasts with pasta sauce and the remaining Parmesan cheese and cook for a further 10 minutes until the chicken is cooked and the cheese is bubbling.
7. When cooking is complete, serve the chicken breasts with courgette.

CHAPTER 9

Snack

Spinach and Crab Meat Cups

MAKES 30 CUPS

| PREP TIME: 10 minutes
| COOK TIME: 8 minutes

1 (170 g) tin crab meat, drained to yield 75 g meat
30 g frozen spinach, thawed, drained, and chopped
1 clove garlic, minced
60 g grated Parmesan cheese
45 ml plain yoghurt
1 ml lemon juice
2 ml Worcestershire sauce
30 mini frozen phyllo shells, thawed
Cooking spray

1. Remove any bits of shell that might remain in the crab meat.
2. Mix the crab meat, spinach, garlic, and cheese together.
3. Stir in the yoghurt, lemon juice, and Worcestershire sauce and combine well.
4. Spoon a tsp. of filling into each phyllo shell.
5. When ready to cook, remove the grill plates and preheat the airfryer baskets for three minutes by activating the automatic preheat key.
6. Place half the shells in each basket and spray with cooking spray. Select the Match Cook key then set basket 1 to 200°C for 8 minutes, then touch the start key to activate the airfryer.
7. When cooking is complete, transfer the shells to a plate. Serve warm.

Mozzarella Arancini

MAKES 16 ARANCINI

| PREP TIME: 5 minutes
| COOK TIME: 12 minutes

30 ml olive oil
400 g cooked rice, cooled
2 eggs, beaten
180 g panko bread crumbs, divided
50 g grated Parmesan cheese
4 g minced fresh basil
16 (2-cm) cubes Mozzarella cheese

1. In a medium bowl, combine the rice, eggs, 60 g of the bread crumbs, Parmesan cheese and basil. Shape this mixture into 16 (4-cm) balls.
2. Poke a hole in each of the balls with your finger and insert a Mozzarella cube. Form the rice mixture firmly around the cheese.
3. On a shallow plate, mix the remaining 120 g of the bread crumbs with the olive oil and combine well. Roll the rice balls in the bread crumbs to coat evenly.
4. When ready to cook, remove the grill plates and preheat the airfryer baskets for three minutes by activating the automatic preheat key.
5. Place half of the arancinis in a single layer in each basket. Select the Match Cook key then set basket 1 to 180°C for 12 minutes, then touch the start key to activate the airfryer. Halfway through cooking, flip the arancinis over.
6. Serve hot.

Dried Pear Slices

SERVES 4

| PREP TIME: 15 minutes
| COOK TIME: 8 hours

15 ml freshly squeezed lemon juice
2 firm Conference pears, cut crosswise into 3-mm-thick slices
½ tsp. ground cinnamon
⅛ tsp. ground cardamom

1. Separate the smaller stem-end pear rounds from the larger rounds with seeds. Remove the core and seeds from the larger slices. Sprinkle all slices with lemon juice, cinnamon and cardamom.
2. Remove the grill plates from the airfryer and divide the slices between the two baskets.
3. Press 1 and select the Dehydrate key, set basket 1 to 60°C for 8 hours. Press 2 and select the Dehydrate key, set basket 2 to 60°C for 8 hours, then touch the start key to activate.
4. When cooking is complete, transfer the slices to a plate and let cool for 30 minutes. Serve immediately.

Crispy Dill Gherkins Slices

MAKES 16 SLICES

| PREP TIME: 5 minutes
| COOK TIME: 7 minutes

Cooking spray
30 g plain flour
50 g panko bread crumbs
2 large dill gherkins, sliced into 8 rounds each
1 large egg, beaten
2 tsps. Cajun seasoning

1. Place the plain flour, panko bread crumbs, and egg into 3 separate shallow bowls, then stir the Cajun seasoning into the flour.
2. Dredge each gherkin slice in the flour mixture, then the egg, and finally the bread crumbs. Shake off any excess, then place each coated gherkin chip on a plate.
3. When ready to cook, remove the grill plates and preheat the airfryer baskets for three minutes by activating the automatic preheat key.
4. Place 8 gherkin slices in a single layer in each basket. Select the Match Cook key then set basket 1 to 200°C for 7 minutes, then touch the start key to activate the airfryer. For even crisping carefully turn the gherkin slices over halfway through cooking using a silicone spatula.
5. When cooking is complete, transfer the gherkin slices to a plate and allow to slightly cool on a wire rack before serving.

Homemade Tortilla Crisps

SERVES 2

| PREP TIME: 5 minutes
| COOK TIME: 5 minutes

15 ml olive oil
8 corn tortillas
salt, to taste

1. Slice the corn tortillas into triangles. Coat with a light brushing of olive oil.
2. When ready to cook, remove the grill plates and preheat the airfryer baskets for three minutes by activating the automatic preheat key.
3. Place half of the tortilla pieces in a single layer in each basket. Select the Match Cook key then set basket 1 to 200°C for 5 minutes, then touch the start key to activate the airfryer. Halfway through cooking, carefully turn the tortilla pieces over.
4. When cooking is complete, transfer the tortilla pieces to a plate. Season with salt before serving.

Cheesy Apple Roll-Ups

MAKES 8 ROLL-UPS

| PREP TIME: 5 minutes
| COOK TIME: 7 minutes

30 g butter, melted
115 g mild cheddar cheese, grated
8 slices whole wheat sandwich bread
½ small apple, chopped

1. Remove the crusts from the bread and flatten the slices with a rolling pin. Don't be gentle. Press hard so that bread will be very thin.
2. Top the bread slices with cheese and chopped apple, dividing the toppings evenly.
3. Roll up each slice tightly and secure each with one or two toothpicks.
4. Brush the outside of rolls with melted butter.
5. Preheat the airfryer baskets with the grill plates inserted for three minutes by activating the automatic preheat key.
6. Place 4 rolls in a single layer in each basket. Select the Match Cook key and set basket 1 to 200°C for 7 minutes and touch the start key to activate.
7. When cooking is complete, transfer the rolls to a plate. Serve warm.

Baked Halloumi Cheese with Greek Salsa

SERVES 4

| PREP TIME: 15 minutes
| COOK TIME: 6 minutes

For the Salsa:
1 small shallot, finely diced
3 garlic cloves, minced
30 ml extra-virgin olive oil
30 ml fresh lemon juice
1 tsp. freshly cracked black pepper
Pinch of coarse salt
1 plum tomato, deseeded and finely diced
75 g finely diced English cucumber
2 tsps. chopped fresh parsley
1 tsp. snipped fresh oregano
1 tsp. snipped fresh dill
For the Cheese:
225 g Halloumi cheese, sliced into 1-cm-thick pieces
15 ml extra-virgin olive oil

1. Combine the shallot, garlic, lemon juice, olive oil, pepper and salt in a medium bowl. Add the cucumber, tomato, dill, parsley and oregano. Toss gently to combine; set aside.
2. Put the cheese slices in a medium bowl. Drizzle with the olive oil. Toss to coat well.
3. Preheat the basket 1 with the grill plate inserted for three minutes by activating the automatic preheat key.
4. Place the cheese into basket 1 and set the temperature to 190°C for 6 minutes then touch the start key to activate the airfryer.
5. When cooking is complete, remove the basket from unit. Divide the cheese among four serving plates. Top with the salsa and serve immediately.

Beef and Mango Skewers

SERVES 4

| PREP TIME: 10 minutes
| COOK TIME: 10 minutes

340 g beef sirloin tip, cut into 2.5 cm cubes
1 mango
15 ml olive oil
15 ml honey
30 ml balsamic vinegar
½ tsp. dried marjoram
Pinch of salt
Freshly ground black pepper, to taste

1. Put the beef cubes in a medium bowl and add the olive oil, honey, balsamic vinegar, marjoram, salt and black pepper. Mix well, then massage the marinade into the beef with your hands. Set aside.
2. To prepare the mango, stand it on end and cut the skin off, using a sharp knife. Then carefully cut around the oval pit to remove the flesh. Cut the mango into 2.5-cm cubes.
3. Thread the metal skewers alternating with three beef cubes and two mango cubes.
4. When ready to cook, remove the grill plate from basket 1 then preheat the airfryer basket for three minutes by activating the automatic preheat key.
5. Put the skewers into basket 1 and set the temperature to 180°C for 10 minutes then touch the start key to activate the airfryer. Halfway through cooking, carefully turn the skewers over.
6. When cooking is complete, transfer the skewers to a plate. Serve warm.

Root Veggie Chips with Herb Salt

SERVES 2

| PREP TIME: 10 minutes
| COOK TIME: 16 minutes

Cooking spray
1 parsnip, washed
1 small beetroot, washed
1 small turnip, washed
½ small sweet potato, washed
5 ml olive oil
Herb Salt:
¼ tsp. coarse salt
2 tsps. finely chopped fresh parsley

1. In a medium bowl, toss the beef with the pasta sauce to coat evenly.
2. In a shallow bowl, combine the bread crumbs, oil and marjoram, and mix well. Drop the beef cubes, one at a time, into the bread crumb mixture to coat thoroughly.
3. When ready to cook, remove the grill plates and preheat the airfryer baskets for three minutes by activating the automatic preheat key.
4. Place half the beef in each basket. Select the Match CooaPeel and thinly slice the parsnip, beetroot, turnip, and sweet potato, then place the vegetables in a large bowl, add the olive oil and toss well.
5. When ready to cook, remove the grill plates and preheat the airfryer baskets for three minutes by activating the automatic preheat key.
6. Place half of the vegetables in a single layer in each basket and spray with cooking spray. Select the Match Cook key then set basket 1 to 200°C for 16 minutes, then touch the start key to activate the airfryer. Halfway through cooking, give the vegetables a shake.
7. While the chips cook, make the herb salt in a small bowl by combining the coarse salt and parsley.
8. When cooking is complete, transfer the chips to a serving plate, then sprinkle the herb salt on top and let cool for 2 to 3 minutes before serving.k key then set basket 1 to 180°C for 14 minutes, then touch the start key to activate the airfryer. Halfway through cooking, give the beef a shake.
9. When cooking is complete, transfer the beef to a plate. Serve hot.

Breaded Beef Cubes

SERVES 4

| PREP TIME: 10 minutes
| COOK TIME: 14 minutes

450 g sirloin tip, cut into 2.5-cm cubes
240 ml cheese pasta sauce
100 g soft bread crumbs
30 ml olive oil
½ tsp. dried marjoram

1. In a medium bowl, toss the beef with the pasta sauce to coat evenly.
2. In a shallow bowl, combine the bread crumbs, oil and marjoram, and mix well. Drop the beef cubes, one at a time, into the bread crumb mixture to coat thoroughly.
3. When ready to cook, remove the grill plates and preheat the airfryer baskets for three minutes by activating the automatic preheat key.
4. Place half the beef in each basket. Select the Match Cook key then set basket 1 to 180°C for 14 minutes, then touch the start key to activate the airfryer. Halfway through cooking, give the beef a shake.
5. When cooking is complete, transfer the beef to a plate. Serve hot.

CHAPTER 10

Dessert

Vanilla Chocolate Balls

SERVES 8

| PREP TIME: 15 minutes
| COOK TIME: 13 minutes

cooking spray
250 g plain flour
170 g chilled butter
45 g chocolate, chopped into 8 chunks
60 g icing sugar
15 g cocoa powder
1 tsp. vanilla extract
Pinch of ground cinnamon

1. Mix the flour, cocoa powder, icing sugar, cinnamon and vanilla extract in a bowl.
2. Add the cold butter and buttermilk and mix until a smooth dough is formed.
3. Divide the dough into 8 equal balls and press 1 chocolate chunk in the centre of each ball. Cover completely with the dough.
4. When ready to cook, remove the grill plates and preheat the airfryer baskets for three minutes by activating the automatic preheat key.
5. Place 4 balls in a single layer in each basket and spray with cooking spray. Select the Match Cook key then set basket 1 to 180°C for 13 minutes, then touch the start key to activate the airfryer. Halfway through cooking, carefully flip the balls over.
6. When cooking is complete, transfer the balls to a plate. Serve warm.

Chocolate Molten Cake

SERVES 4

| PREP TIME: 5 minutes
| COOK TIME: 12 minutes

100 g butter, melted
2 eggs
100 g chocolate, melted
45 g sugar
12 g flour

1. Grease four 7-cm ramekins with a little butter.
2. Rigorously combine the eggs, butter and sugar before stirring in the melted chocolate. Slowly fold in the flour.
3. Spoon an equal amount of the mixture into each ramekin.
4. When ready to cook, remove the grill plates and preheat the airfryer baskets for three minutes by activating the automatic preheat key.
5. Place 2 ramekins in each basket. Select the Match Cook key then set basket 1 to 180°C for 12 minutes, then touch the start key to activate the airfryer.
6. When cooking is complete, put the ramekins upside-down on plates and let the cakes fall out. Serve warm.

Chocolate Yoghurt Pecans Muffins

SERVES 8

| PREP TIME: 15 minutes
| COOK TIME: 15 minutes

180 g plain flour
240 ml yoghurt
30 g pecans, chopped
45 g mini chocolate chips
50 g sugar
10 g baking powder
80 ml vegetable oil
½ tsp. salt
2 tsps. vanilla extract

1. Grease 8 muffin moulds lightly.
2. Mix the flour, sugar, baking powder, and salt in a bowl.
3. Combine the yoghurt, oil, and vanilla extract in another bowl.
4. Fold in the chocolate chips and pecans and divide the mixture into the muffin moulds.
5. When ready to cook, remove the grill plates and preheat the airfryer baskets for three minutes by activating the automatic preheat key.
6. Place 4 muffin moulds in a single layer in each basket. Select the Match Cook key then set basket 1 to 180°C for 15 minutes, then touch the start key to activate the airfryer.
7. When cooking is complete, remove the muffin moulds from airfryer and invert the muffins onto wire rack to cool completely before serving.

Air Fried Bananas

SERVES 6

| PREP TIME: 5 minutes
| COOK TIME: 7 minutes

30 g plain bread crumbs
30 g cornflour
1 large egg
3 bananas, halved crosswise
cooking oil
chocolate sauce, for drizzling

1. In a small bowl, beat the egg. In another bowl, add the cornflour. Place the bread crumbs in a third bowl.
2. Dip the bananas in the cornflour, then the egg, and then the bread crumbs.
3. When ready to cook, remove the grill plate from basket 1 then preheat the airfryer basket for three minutes by activating the automatic preheat key.
4. Spray the basket with cooking oil and place bananas in basket 1. Set the temperature to 180°C for 7 minutes then touch the start key to activate the airfryer. Halfway through cooking, carefully flip the bananas over.
5. When cooking is complete, transfer the bananas to a plate. Drizzle the chocolate sauce over the bananas and serve hot.

Chocolate Lover's Muffins

SERVES 8

| PREP TIME: 10 minutes
| COOK TIME: 15 minutes

180 g plain flour
1 egg
240 ml yoghurt
90 g mini chocolate chips
50 g sugar
10 g baking powder
80 ml vegetable oil
2 tsps. vanilla extract
salt, to taste

1. Grease 8 muffin cups lightly.
2. Mix the flour, baking powder, sugar and salt in a bowl.
3. Whisk egg, yoghurt, oil and vanilla extract in another bowl.
4. Combine the flour and egg mixtures and mix until a smooth mixture is formed.
5. Fold in the chocolate chips and divide this mixture evenly into the prepared muffin cups.
6. When ready to cook, remove the grill plates and preheat the airfryer baskets for three minutes by activating the automatic preheat key.
7. Place 4 muffin cups in a single layer in each basket. Select the Match Cook key then set basket 1 to 180°C for 15 minutes, then touch the start key to activate the airfryer.
8. When cooking is complete, refrigerate for 2 hours and serve chilled.

Chocolate Coconut Brownies

SERVES 8

| PREP TIME: 15 minutes
| COOK TIME: 15 minutes

120 ml coconut oil
60 g dark chocolate
200 g sugar
4 whisked eggs
35 ml water
½ tsp. ground star anise
½ tsp. vanilla extract

¼ tsp. coconut extract
¼ tsp. ground cinnamon
15 ml honey
60 g desiccated coconut
60 g flour
sugar, for dusting

1. Melt the coconut oil and dark chocolate in the microwave.
2. Combine with the sugar, eggs, cinnamon, anise, water, coconut extract, vanilla, and honey in a large bowl.
3. Stir in the flour and desiccated coconut. Incorporate everything well.
4. Lightly grease a 18x13 cm baking tin with butter. Transfer the mixture to the tin.
5. When ready to cook, remove the grill plate from basket 1 then preheat the airfryer basket for three minutes by activating the automatic preheat key.
6. Place the baking tin in basket 1 and set the temperature to 180°C for 15 minutes then touch the start key to activate the airfryer.
7. When cooking is complete, remove the baking tin from the airfryer and allow to cool slightly. Slice it into squares and dust with sugar before serving

Peach Parcel

SERVES 2

| PREP TIME: 10 minutes
| COOK TIME: 15 minutes

240 ml prepared vanilla custard
1 peach, peeled, cored and halved
2 puff pastry sheets
1 egg, beaten lightly
15 g sugar
Pinch of ground cinnamon
15 ml whipped cream

1. Place a spoonful of custard and a peach half in the centre of each pastry sheet.
2. Mix the sugar and cinnamon in a bowl and sprinkle on the peach halves.
3. Pinch the corners of sheets together to shape into a parcel.
4. When ready to cook, remove the grill plate from basket 1 then preheat the airfryer basket for three minutes by activating the automatic preheat key.
5. Put the parcels into basket 1 and set the temperature to 170°C for 15 minutes then touch the start key to activate the airfryer.
6. When cooking is complete, transfer the parcels to a plate. Top with whipped cream. Serve with remaining custard.

Crispy Berries Tacos

SERVES 2

| PREP TIME: 5 minutes
| COOK TIME: 6 minutes

cooking spray
2 soft shell tortillas
30 g raspberries
30 g blueberries
60 g strawberry jam
15 g icing sugar

1. Put 30 g strawberry jam over each tortilla and top with blueberries and raspberries. Sprinkle lightly with icing sugar.
2. When ready to cook, remove the grill plate from basket 1 then preheat the airfryer basket for three minutes by activating the automatic preheat key.
3. Put the tortillas into basket 1 and spray with cooking spray. Set the temperature to 150°C for 6 minutes then touch the start key to activate the airfryer.
4. When cooking is complete, transfer the tortillas to a plate. Serve warm.

Walnut Fudge Muffins

SERVES 10

| PREP TIME: 5 minutes
| COOK TIME: 12 minutes

1 package fudge brownie mix
1 egg
30 ml water
30 g walnuts, chopped
80 ml vegetable oil

1. Grease 10 muffin tins lightly.
2. Mix the brownie mix, egg, oil and water in a medium bowl.
3. Fold in the walnuts and pour the mixture in the muffin cups.
4. When ready to cook, remove the grill plates and preheat the airfryer baskets for three minutes by activating the automatic preheat key.
5. Place half of the muffin cups in a single layer in each basket. Select the Match Cook key then set basket 1 to 150°C for 12 minutes, then touch the start key to activate the airfryer.
6. When cooking is complete, dish out and serve immediately.

Bourbon Monkey Bread

SERVES 6

| PREP TIME: 15 minutes
| COOK TIME: 25 minutes

1 (460 g) tin store-bought refrigerated biscuit dough
50 g packed light brown sugar
60 g icing sugar
55 g unsalted butter, melted
1 tsp. ground cinnamon
½ tsp. ground ginger
½ tsp. freshly grated nutmeg
½ tsp. coarse salt
¼ tsp. ground allspice
⅛ tsp. ground cloves
10 ml bourbon
15 g chopped pecans
30 g chopped candied cherries

1. Open the tin and separate the biscuits, then cut each into quarters. Toss the biscuit quarters in a large bowl with the brown sugar, ginger, cinnamon, nutmeg, salt, allspice and cloves until evenly coated.
2. Transfer the dough pieces and any sugar left in the bowl into a 7-cm round cake pan and coat evenly with the melted butter.
3. When ready to cook, remove the grill plate from basket 1 then preheat the airfryer basket for three minutes by activating the automatic preheat key.
4. Put the cake pan into basket 1 and set the temperature to 150°C for 25 minutes then touch the start key to activate the airfryer. Bake until the monkey bread is golden brown and cooked through in the middle.
5. When cooking is complete, transfer the pan to a wire rack and let cool completely. Unmould from the pan.
6. In a small bowl, whisk the icing sugar and bourbon into a smooth glaze. Drizzle the glaze over the cooled monkey bread and, while the glaze is still wet, sprinkle with the cherries and pecans to serve.

Appendix 1: Tower Vortx Dual Basket Pre-set Menu Table

The table below shows the pre-set times and cooking temperatures for each of the unit's 12 auto-cook menus.

PRE-SET FUNCTIONS	DEFAULT TIME	DEFAULT TEMP (°C)
PRE-HEAT	3 mins	180°C
FRIES	18 mins	200°C
MEAT	12 mins	200°C
DRUMSTICKS	20 mins	200°C
STEAK	12 mins	180°C
CAKE	25 mins	160°C
PRAWN	8 mins	180°C
FISH	10 mins	180°C
PIZZA	20 mins	180°C
VEGETABLES	10 mins	160°C
RE-HEAT	15 mins	150°C
DEHYDRATE	6 hrs Adjustable time: 0.5 hr to 24 hrs	60°C

Appendix 2: Recipes Index

Printed in Great Britain
by Amazon

28057072R00044